AF599241

St. Joseph Daily Prayer Book

"Alleluia. The Lord our powerful God is King; let us rejoice, sing praise, and give him glory. Alleluia."

ST. JOSEPH DAILY PRAYER BOOK

PRAYERS, READINGS, AND DEVOTIONS FOR THE YEAR

Including Morning and Evening Prayer from the "Liturgy of the Hours"

(1st Week—Slightly Abridged)

CATHOLIC BOOK PUBLISHING CORP.
New Jersey

NIHIL OBSTAT: Francis J. McAree, S.T.D.
Censor Librorum

IMPRIMATUR: ✠ Patrick J. Sheridan, D.D.
Vicar General, Archdiocese of New York

(T-142)

ISBN 978-0-89942-142-1

Printed in China 25 HA 2

catholicbookpublishing.com

CONTENTS

INTRODUCTION

THE most important prayer of the Church is the Mass. No one doubts that, but what is the second most important prayer of the Church? Benediction? The Rosary? Stations of the Cross? No, the second most important prayer of the Church is the Breviary or the Liturgy of the Hours, also called the Divine Office.

Praying the Breviary used to be the exclusive prayer of priests and religious, but it truly belongs to all the Church. Many Catholics are discovering the richness and beauty of praying the Liturgy of the Hours. It has regained its proper place as the public prayer of all the Church.

This prayer book proudly contains a slightly abridged form of Morning and Evening prayer from the first week of the Breviary. The Church heartily recommends Morning and Evening prayer for all believers as the two most important hours in the Liturgy of the Hours. Praying the Breviary can be particularly helpful to people who find prayer difficult.

The Church designed the Liturgy of the Hours to be prayed with others. The document to introduce the Breviary emphasizes the importance of praying as a community. "Like the other Liturgical actions, the Liturgy of the Hours is not a private action but pertains to the whole Body of the Church. It manifests the Church and has an effect upon it."

The family is the domestic church, and praying the Liturgy of the Hours together can add so much to your life as a family. In many families today, finding time to pray together is so difficult. Praying the Liturgy of the Hours together can transform your entire family life. You will become more focused on the place of God in your family and can set a spiritual tone for everyone. Prayer is also a terrific way to teach your children the importance of faith and prayer. Decide for your own good to pray Morning and Evening prayer together every day. It gives your family regular time together, free from so many distractions.

This is especially true of married couples. In any marriage, the husband and wife are called to help each other become more Christ-like and show each other they are keeping Christ present and alive in their lives. This is difficult to do without praying together as a couple. Praying the Breviary together can be a powerful tool to strengthen the communication. The Breviary takes communicating to a deeper, spiritual level. It commits you, not just to a healthy marriage, but to a healthy spiritual life. Just as the family that prays together, stays together, so too, the couple that prays together has a better chance of staying together.

Even when praying your office alone, unite yourselves with Christians in every land as they also pray their Morning and Evening prayer. Unite your minds and voices with millions of men and women throughout the world who also pray the Breviary.

The Psalms are the heart of the Divine Office. Morning and Evening prayer begins with singing God's praises. Every Psalm includes an Antiphon that should be recited at the start of the Psalm and repeated at the Psalm's conclusion. Also, end each Psalm by praying the *Glory Be*. When we pray with someone else, alternate the reading of the verses of the different Psalms.

The Liturgy of the Hours is made up almost entirely from the Bible. After praying the Psalms, we read a short passage from Scriptures. Allow God to speak to you through your prayerful and meditative reading of the Scriptures. But rather than read every week the same reading selected in this prayer book, allow for more variety. Pick a book from the Bible that appeals to you and read from it every day. When you have finished one book, start another. If you pray the Breviary with someone else, after the reading, share your own thoughts and reflections on what you have heard.

Then we pray together a Gospel canticle, the *Canticle of Zechariah* at Morning prayer and the *Canticle of Mary* at Evening prayer.

The Church includes specific intercessions, to which we should add our own prayers for our family and other concerns. I would also suggest that you write on an index card any intentions that are close to your heart. Then include them at this time every day. Never be afraid of asking God for His grace in prayer. The persistent, consistent person will grow in faith and the Holy Spirit.

We conclude our Morning and Evening prayer with an *Our Father* and a closing prayer.

Sanctify your whole day by beginning the day with Morning prayer and ending the day with Evening prayer. Become one with believers throughout the world in praying this ancient form of Christian prayer.

Father John Murray, C.Ss.R.

MOST USED PRAYERS

Angelus

Leader: The angel of the Lord declared unto Mary,

All: And she conceived of the Holy Spirit.

Hail Mary . . .

Leader: Behold the handmaid of the Lord.

All: Be it done to me according to your word.

Hail Mary . . .

Leader: The word was made flesh,

All: And dwelt amongst us.

Hail Mary . . .

Leader: Pray for us, O holy mother of God,

All: That we may be made worthy of the promises of Christ.

Leader: Let us pray. Pour forth, we beseech you, O Lord, your grace into our hearts, that we, to whom the incarnation of Christ your Son was made known by the message of an angel, may by his passion and cross be brought to the glory of his Resurrection through Christ, Our Lord.

All: Amen.

Queen of Heaven

During the Easter Season:

Leader: Queen of Heaven, rejoice, alleluia.

All: The Son whom you were privileged to bear, alleluia, has risen as he said, alleluia. Pray to God for us, alleluia.

Leader: Rejoice and be glad, Virgin Mary, alleluia.

All: For the Lord has truly risen, alleluia.

Leader: Let us pray. O God, it was by the Resurrection of your Son, our Lord Jesus Christ, that you brought joy to the world. Grant that through the intercession of the Virgin Mary, his mother, we may attain the joy of eternal life. Through Christ our Lord.

All: Amen.

Blessing before Meals

BLESS us, O Lord, and these your gifts, which we are about to receive from your bounty through Christ our Lord. Amen.

Grace after Meals

WE give you thanks for all your benefits, O almighty God, who live and reign forever and ever. Amen.

May the souls of all the faithful departed through the mercy of God rest in peace. Amen.

Invocations

May the Holy Trinity be blessed.

* * *

Christ conquers! Christ reigns! Christ commands!

* * *

O Heart of Jesus, burning with love for us, inflame our hearts with love for you.

* * *

O Heart of Jesus, I place my trust in you.

* * *

O Heart of Jesus, all for you.

* * *

Most Sacred Heart of Jesus, have mercy on us.

* * *

My God and my all.

* * *

Jesus, meek and humble of heart, make my heart like your Heart. *(Roman Ritual)*

* * *

May the Most Blessed Sacrament be praised and adored forever.

* * *

Jesus, Mary, Joseph, I give you my heart and my soul.

Jesus, Mary, Joseph, assist me in my last agony.

Jesus, Mary, Joseph, may I sleep and rest in peace with you. *(Roman Ritual)*

* * *

Sweet Heart of Mary, be my salvation.

* * *

Pray for us, O Holy Mother of God, that we may be made worthy of the promises of Christ. *(Roman Ritual)*

* * *

Queen conceived without original sin, pray for us who have recourse to you.

THE PSALTER

The Psalms are the prayer of God's assembly, the public prayer par excellence of the people of God. They recall to mind the truths revealed by God to the chosen people; they keep repeating and fostering the hope of the promised Redeemer, and they show forth in splendid light the prophesied glory of Jesus Christ.

In a similar way they express the joy, the bitterness, the hope and fear of our hearts and our desire of loving God and hoping in him alone, and our mystic ascent to divine tabernacles.

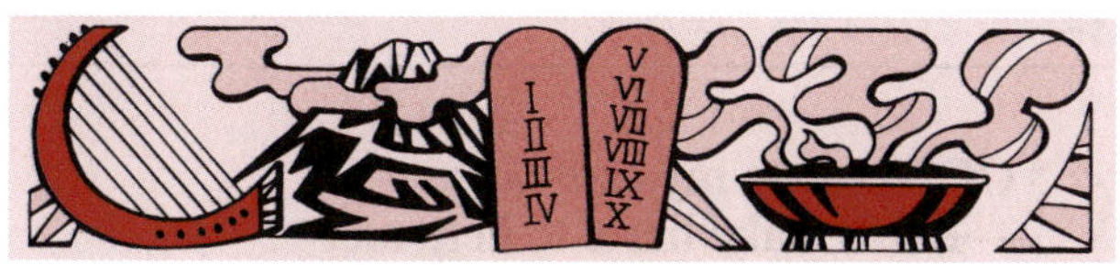

SUNDAY EVENING I

Reflection

PSALM 141 is one of the Church's traditional evening prayers. It is a prayer we can all say, Saint Augustine observes, for it is a prayer of the body of Christ, the Church. Sometimes Christ prays in his Church as she is in anguish; sometimes he prays in us as we rejoice. But we are never alone in prayer. Christ has made us his own, and so we share in his life, his merits, and his prayer.

The incense we offer, the evening oblation we make is the passion of the Lord. "When day was fading into evening, the Lord laid down his life on the cross," Saint Augustine says; "in his resurrection he made this evening sacrifice a morning offering."

As this day ends, our own offering to God is made with that of Christ's. His merits and prayers make what we do acceptable before God, the Father. Our lives this day are brought to the Father through him.

So it is that "at the name of Jesus every knee should bend of those in heaven, and on earth and under the earth, and every tongue should proclaim to the glory of God the Father: Jesus Christ is Lord" (Colossians 2:10-11).

EVENING PRAYER I

GOD, come to my assistance.
—Lord, make haste to help me.
Glory to the Father, and to the Son, and to the Holy Spirit:
—as it was in the beginning, is now, and will be for ever. Amen. Alleluia.

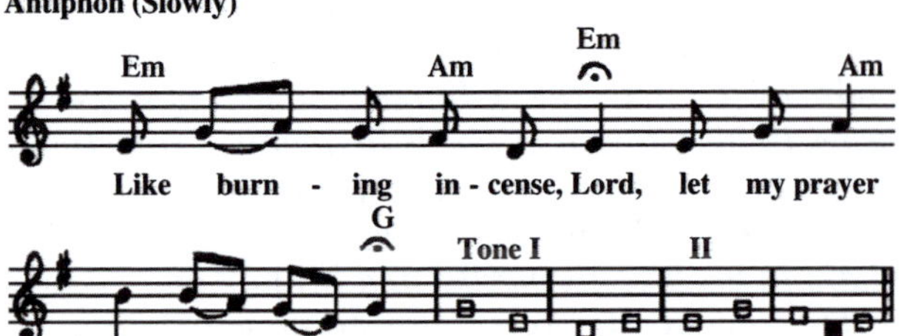

Psalm 141:1-9

A prayer when in danger

An angel stood before the face of God, thurible in hand. The fragrant incense soaring aloft was the prayer of God's people on earth (Revelation 8:4).

I HAVE called to you, Lord; hasten to help me!
Hear my voice when I cry to you.
Let my prayer arise before you like incense,
the raising of my hands like an evening oblation.

Set, O Lord, a guard over my mouth;
keep watch at the door of my lips!

Do not turn my heart to things that are wrong,
to evil deeds with men who are sinners.

Never allow me to share in their feasting.
If a good man strikes or reproves me it is kindness;
but let the oil of the wicked not anoint my head.
Let my prayer be ever against their malice.

Their princes were thrown down by the side of the rock:
then they understood that my words were kind.
As a millstone is shattered to pieces on the ground,
so their bones were strewn at the mouth of the grave.

To you, Lord God, my eyes are turned:
in you I take refuge; spare my soul!
From the trap they have laid for me keep me safe:
keep me from the snares of those who do evil.

Glory to the Father, and to the Son, and to the Holy Spirit:
as it was in the beginning, is now, and will be for ever. Amen.

Psalm-prayer

Lord, from the rising of the sun to its setting your name is worthy of all praise. Let our prayer come like incense before you. May the lifting up of our hands be as an evening sacrifice acceptable to you, Lord our God.

Psalm 142

You, Lord, are my refuge

What is written in this psalm was fulfilled in our Lord's passion (Saint Hilary).

WITH all my voice I cry to the Lord,
with all my voice I entreat the Lord.
I pour out my trouble before him;
I tell him all my distress
while my spirit faints within me.
But you, O Lord, know my path.

On the way where I shall walk
they have hidden a snare to entrap me.
Look on my right and see:
there is not one who takes my part.
I have no means of escape,
not one who cares for my soul.

I cry to you, O Lord.
I have said: "You are my refuge,

all I have left in the land of the living."
Listen then to my cry
for I am in the depths of distress.

Rescue me from those who pursue me
for they are stronger than I.
Bring my soul out of this prison
and then I shall praise your name.
Around me the just will assemble
because of your goodness to me.

Glory to the Father, and to the Son, and to the Holy Spirit:
as it was in the beginning, is now, and will be for ever. Amen.

Psalm-prayer

Lord, we humbly ask for your goodness. May you help us to hope in you, and give us a share with your chosen ones in the land of the living.

Reading

Romans 11: 33-36

HOW rich are the depths of God—how deep his wisdom and knowledge—and how impossible to penetrate his motives or understand his methods! Who could ever know the mind of the Lord? Who could ever be his counselor? Who could ever give him anything or lend him anything? All that exists comes from him; all is by him and for him. To him be glory for ever! Amen.

Responsory

Our hearts are filled with wonder, as we contemplate your works, O Lord.

—Our hearts are filled with wonder, as we contemplate your works, O Lord.
We praise the wisdom which wrought them all,
—as we contemplate your works, O Lord.
Glory to the Father, and to the Son, and to the Holy Spirit.
—Our hearts are filled with wonder, as we contemplate your works, O Lord.

Antiphon

My spirit rejoices in God my Savior.*

Canticle of Mary

The soul rejoices in the Lord

MY SOUL proclaims the greatness of the Lord,
my spirit rejoices in God my Savior
for he has looked with favor on his lowly servant.

From this day all generations will call me blessed:
the Almighty has done great things for me,
and holy is his Name.

He has mercy on those who fear him
in every generation.

He has shown the strength of his arm,
he has scattered the proud in their conceit.

He has cast down the mighty from their thrones,
and has lifted up the lowly.

* Proper antiphon for Tuesday, Week I.

He has filled the hungry with good things
and the rich he has sent away empty.

He has come to the help of his servant Israel
for he has remembered his promise of mercy,
the promise he made to our fathers,
to Abraham and his children for ever.

Glory to the Father, and to the Son, and to the Holy Spirit:
as it was in the beginning, is now, and will be for ever. Amen.

(For music, turn to p. 132)

Intercessions

WE GIVE glory to the one God—Father, Son and Holy Spirit—and in our weakness we pray:
Lord, be with your people.

Holy Lord, Father all-powerful, let justice spring up on the earth,
—then your people will dwell in the beauty of peace.

Let every nation come into your kingdom,
—so that all peoples will be saved.

Let married couples live in your peace,
—and grow in mutual love.

Reward all who have done good to us, Lord,
—and grant them eternal life.

Look with compassion on victims of hatred and war,
—grant them heavenly peace.

Our Father . . .

Prayer

(16th Sun. Ord. Time)

FATHER,
let the gift of your life
continue to grow in us,
drawing us from death to faith, hope, and love.
Keep us alive in Christ Jesus.
Keep us watchful in prayer
and true to his teaching
till your glory is revealed in us.

Grant this through Christ our Lord.

(Dismissal, p. 133)

SUNDAY MORNING

Reflection

The prayers for morning and evening begin with some verses from the Psalms:

Lord, open my lips.
—And my mouth will proclaim your praise.
God, come to my assistance.
—Lord, make haste to help me.

Prayer is a gift—God's gift—these opening verses say. Unless he opens our lips and comes to our assistance, we cannot pray.

"Ask, and you will receive. Seek, and you will find. Knock, and it will be opened to you" (Matthew 7:7). *If we come to prayer like beggars—thirsty, hungry and poor—then God will spread his gifts before us. If we come before him forgetful of ourselves, open and expectant, then he will open our eyes to the wonders of life.*

Unless God helps us, we may settle down like the Pharisee, congratulating ourselves on our pocketful of small achievements (Luke 18:9ff), *or like the rich fool, mistaking the few barns we possess for the world. "God, come to my assistance." "Lord, open my lips."*

Psalm 149 and the reading from Revelation (7:9-12) add the song of all creation to our own limited song. United with everything and everyone on earth as well as with the saints in heaven, we praise God through Jesus Christ, from whom all life comes.

MORNING PRAYER

LORD, open my lips.
—And my mouth will proclaim your praise.
Glory to, etc.: —as it was, etc.

Antiphon

Come, let us sing to the Lord, and shout with joy to the Rock who saves us, alleluia.

Invitatory psalm, p. 126.

Antiphon

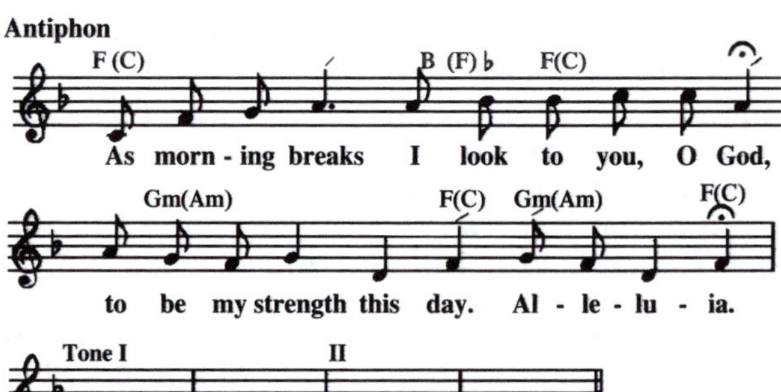

Psalm 63:2-9

A soul thirsting for God

Whoever has left the darkness of sin, yearns for God.

O GOD, you are my God for you I long;
for you my soul is thirsting.
My body pines for you
like a dry, weary land without water.
So I gaze on you in the sanctuary
to see your strength and your glory.

For your love is better than life,
my lips will speak your praise.
So I will bless you all my life,
in your name I will lift up my hands.
My soul shall be filled as with a banquet,
my mouth shall praise you with joy.

On my bed I remember you.
On you I muse through the night
for you have been my help;
in the shadow of your wings I rejoice.
My soul clings to you;
your right hand holds me fast.

Glory to the Father, and to the Son, and to the Holy Spirit:
as it was in the beginning, is now, and will be for ever. Amen.

Psalm-prayer

Father, creator of unfailing light, give that same light to those who call to you. May our lips praise you; our lives proclaim your goodness; our work give you honor, and our voices celebrate you for ever.

Antiphon

Psalm 149

The joy of God's holy people

Let the sons of the Church, the children of the new people, rejoice in Christ, their King (Hesychius).

SING a new song to the Lord,
his praise in the assembly of the faithful.
Let Israel rejoice in its maker,
let Zion's sons exult in their king.
Let them praise his name with dancing
and make music with timbrel and harp.

For the Lord takes delight in his people.
He crowns the poor with salvation.
Let the faithful rejoice in their glory,
shout for joy and take their rest.
Let the praise of God be on their lips
and a two-edged sword in their hand,

to deal out vengeance to the nations
and punishment on all the peoples;
to bind their kings in chains
and their nobles in fetters of iron;
to carry out the sentence pre-ordained;
this honor is for all his faithful.

Glory to the Father, and to the Son, and to the Holy Spirit:
as it was in the beginning, is now, and will be for ever. Amen.

Psalm-prayer

Let Israel rejoice in you, Lord, and acknowledge you as creator and redeemer. We put our trust in your faithfulness and proclaim the wonderful truths of salvation. May your loving kindness embrace us now and for ever.

Reading

Revelation 7: 9-12

AFTER that I saw a huge number, impossible to count, of people from every nation, race, tribe and language; they were standing in front of the throne and in front of the Lamb, dressed in white robes and holding palms in their hands. They shouted aloud, "Victory to our God, who sits on the throne, and to the Lamb!" And all the angels who were standing in a circle around the throne, surrounding the elders and the four animals, prostrated themselves before the throne, and touched the ground with their foreheads, worshiping God with these words, "Amen. Praise and glory and wisdom and thanksgiving and honor and power and strength to our God for ever and ever. Amen."

Responsory

Christ, Son of the living God, have mercy on us.
—Christ, Son of the living God, have mercy on us.
You are seated at the right hand of the Father,
—have mercy on us.
Glory to the Father, and to the Son, and to the Holy Spirit.
—Christ, Son of the living God, have mercy on us.

Antiphon

Lord, guide our feet into the way of peace.*

Canticle of Zechariah

The Messiah and his forerunner

BLESSED be the Lord, the God of Israel;
he has come to his people and set them free.

He has raised up for us a mighty savior,
born of the house of his servant David.

Through his holy prophets he promised of old
that he would save us from our enemies,
from the hands of all who hate us.

He promised to show mercy to our fathers
and to remember his holy covenant.

This was the oath he swore to our father Abraham:
to set us free from the hands of our enemies,
free to worship him without fear,
holy and righteous in his sight
all the days of our life.

You, my child, shall be called the prophet of the Most High;
for you will go before the Lord to prepare his way,
to give his people knowledge of salvation
by the forgiveness of their sins.

*Proper antiphon for Saturday, Week IV.

In the tender compassion of our God
the dawn from on high shall break upon us,
to shine on those who dwell in darkness and the shadow of death,
and to guide our feet into the way of peace.

Glory to the Father, and to the Son, and to the Holy Spirit:
as it was in the beginning, is now, and will be for ever. Amen.

(For music, turn to p. 131)

Intercessions

CHRIST is the sun that never sets, the true light that shines on every man. Let us call out to him in praise:
Lord, you are our life and our salvation.
Creator of the stars, we thank you for your gift, the first rays of the dawn,
—and we commemorate your resurrection.
May your Holy Spirit teach us to do your will today,
—and may your Wisdom guide us always.
Each Sunday give us the joy of gathering as your people,
—around the table of your Word and your Body.
From our hearts we thank you,
—for your countless blessings.

Our Father . . .

Prayer

(18th Sun. Ord. Time)

GOD our Father,
gifts without measure flow from your goodness
to bring us your peace.
Our life is your gift.
Guide our life's journey,
for only your love makes us whole.
Keep us strong in your love.

We ask this through Christ our Lord.

(Dismissal, p. 133)

SUNDAY EVENING II

Reflection

EVERY Sunday we celebrate the Resurrection of Christ. Not only did Jesus rise from the dead but he ascended to his heavenly Father, who gave him all power in heaven and on earth.

In Psalm 110, a Psalm originally celebrating the day an ancient Israelite king was enthroned amid the joy of his people, we express our faith in the Resurrection of Jesus and his kingship. We celebrate the homecoming of Christ, our Lord.

Before all creation, the Father proclaims the rule of his Son. Like a warrior who has earned his victory, Jesus Christ holds in his hands our yesterdays, todays, and tomorrows. His power flows surely and unceasingly through all time and space.

"A priest, like Melchizedek of old," Jesus Christ offers to his Father a world which is dear to him. A compassionate priest, he knows the sufferings and aspirations of humanity.

A homecoming as well as an enthronement is described in Psalm 110. Can we not know in this Psalm the Father's touching, welcoming embrace of his Son, and his ready acceptance of all that is human through his Son's humanity? Can we not see his eyes softening gently at the sight of his wounds? Can God be unmindful of any human grief and suffering since he has tasted it so deeply in the sufferings of Christ?

An ancient people once sang Psalm 110 rejoicing on the day of their king's enthronement. Today we rejoice knowing that the reign of Jesus Christ will never end.

Our union with him is described in Psalm 114. We are like Israel: come forth from Egypt. The power of Christ redeems us.

The day of Christ's enthronement is also "the wedding day of the Lamb." All of us, "great and small," are espoused to him who, from his own riches, clothes us in the fine apparel of his grace.

EVENING PRAYER

God, come to my assistance.
—Lord make haste to help me.
Glory to the Father, and to the Son, and to the Holy Spirit:
—as it was in the beginning, is now, and will be for ever. Amen. Alleluia.

Antiphon

Psalm 110:1-5, 7

The Messiah, king and priest

Christ's reign will last until all his enemies are made subject to him (1 Corinthians 15:25).

THE Lord's revelation to my Master:
"Sit on my right:
your foes I will put beneath your feet."

The Lord will wield from Zion
your scepter of power:
rule in the midst of all your foes.

A prince from the day of your birth
on the holy mountains;
from the womb before the dawn I begot you.

The Lord has sworn an oath he will not change.
"You are a priest for ever,
a priest like Melchizedek of old."

The Master standing at your right hand
will shatter kings in the day of his great wrath.

He shall drink from the stream by the wayside
and therefore he shall lift up his head.

Glory to the Father, and to the Son, and to the Holy Spirit:
as it was in the beginning, is now, and will be for ever. Amen.

Psalm-prayer

Father, we ask you to give us victory and peace. In Jesus Christ, our Lord and King, we are already seated at your right hand. We look forward to praising you in the fellowship of all your saints in our heavenly homeland.

Antiphon

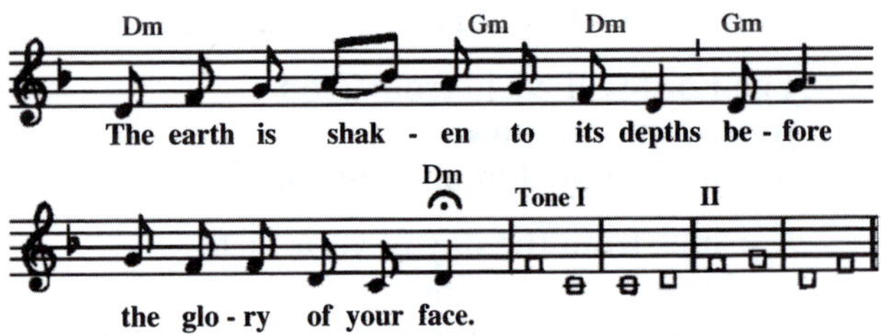

Psalm 114

The Israelites are delivered from the bondage of Egypt

You too left Egypt when, at baptism, you renounced that world which is at enmity with God (Saint Augustine).

WHEN Israel came forth from Egypt,
Jacob's sons from an alien people,
Judah became the Lord's temple,
Israel became his kingdom.

The sea fled at the sight:
the Jordan turned back on its course,
the mountains leapt like rams
and the hills like yearling sheep.

Why was it, sea, that you fled,
that you turned back, Jordan, on your course?
Mountains, that you leapt like rams,
hills, like yearling sheep?

Tremble, O earth, before the Lord,
in the presence of the God of Jacob,
who turns the rock into a pool
and flint into a spring of water.

Glory to the Father, and to the Son, and to the Holy Spirit:
as it was in the beginning, is now, and will be for ever. Amen.

Psalm-prayer

Almighty God, ever-living mystery of unity and Trinity, you gave life to the new Israel by birth from water and the Spirit, and made it a chosen race, a royal priesthood, a people set apart as your eternal possession. May all those you have called to walk in the splendor of the new light render you fitting service and adoration.

Reading

2 Corinthians 1:3-4

BLESSED be the God and Father of our Lord Jesus Christ, a gentle Father and the God of all consolation, who comforts us in all our sorrows, so that we can offer to others, in their sorrows, the consolation that we have received from God ourselves.

Responsory

The whole creation proclaims the greatness of your glory.
—The whole creation proclaims the greatness of your glory.
Eternal ages praise
—the greatness of your glory.

Glory to the Father, and to the Son, and to the Holy Spirit.
—The whole creation proclaims the greatness of your glory.

Antiphon

My spirit rejoices in God my Savior.*

Canticle of Mary

The soul rejoices in the Lord

MY SOUL proclaims the greatness of the Lord,
my spirit rejoices in God my Savior
for he has looked with favor on his lowly servant.

From this day all generations will call me blessed:
the Almighty has done great things for me,
and holy is his Name.

*Proper antiphon for Tuesday, Week I.

He has mercy on those who fear him
in every generation.

He has shown the strength of his arm,
he has scattered the proud in their conceit.

He has cast down the mighty from their thrones,
and has lifted up the lowly.

He has filled the hungry with good things
and the rich he has sent away empty.

He has come to the help of his servant Israel
for he has remembered his promise of mercy,
the promise he made to our fathers,
to Abraham and his children for ever.

Glory to the Father, and to the Son, and to the Holy Spirit:
as it was in the beginning, is now, and will be for ever. Amen.

(For music, turn to p. 132)

Intercessions

CHRIST the Lord is our head; we are his members. In joy let us call out to him:
Lord, may your kingdom come.

Christ our Savior, make your Church a more vivid symbol of the unity of all mankind,
—make it more effectively the sacrament of salvation for all peoples.

Through your presence, guide the college of bishops in union with the Pope,
—give them the gifts of unity, love and peace.

Bind all Christians more closely to yourself; their divine Head,
—lead them to proclaim your kingdom by the witness of their lives.
Grant peace to the world,
—let every land flourish in justice and security.
Grant to the dead the glory of resurrection,
—and give us a share in their happiness.

Our Father . . .

Prayer

(8th Sun. Ord. Time)

FATHER in heaven,
form in us the likeness of your Son
and deepen his life within us.
Send us as witnesses of gospel joy
into a world of fragile peace and broken promises.
Touch the hearts of all men with your love
that they in turn may love one another.

We ask this through Christ our Lord.

(Dismissal, p. 133)

MONDAY MORNING

Reflection

"A GOOD man is always a beginner," wrote the Roman writer, Martial.

Morning prayer can be a good beginning for the day that is ours today.

"We pray in the morning," says the 4th century bishop, Saint Basil, in one of his writings, "so that the first stirrings of our mind and will may be consecrated to God and that we may take nothing in hand until we have been gladdened by the thought of God." He then adds a verse from Psalm 5: "It is you whom I invoke, O Lord. In the morning you hear me."

Yes, we should begin our life today nourished by faith, hope and love. May our hands take up the new work before us and continue what we have begun. May we complete what God gives us to do.

This morning's Psalms, prayers and reading offer us perspective and motivation for the day before us. Whether the circumstances of life are stormy or quiet, may his will be done.

We must never grow weary of doing what is right.

MORNING PRAYER

LORD, open my lips.
—And my mouth will proclaim your praise.
Glory to, etc.: —as it was, etc.

Antiphon

Let us approach the Lord with praise and thanksgiving.

Invitatory psalm, p. 126.

Psalm 5:2-10, 12-13

A morning prayer asking for help

Those who welcome the Word as the guest of their hearts will have abiding joy.

TO MY words give ear, O Lord,
give heed to my groaning.
Attend to the sound of my cries,
my King and my God.

It is you whom I invoke, O Lord.
In the morning you hear me;
in the morning I offer you my prayer,
watching and waiting.

You are no God who loves evil;
no sinner is your guest.
The boastful shall not stand their ground
before your face.

You hate all who do evil:
you destroy all who lie.
The deceitful and bloodthirsty man
the Lord detests.

But I through the greatness of your love
have access to your house.
I bow down before your holy temple,
filled with awe.

Lead me, Lord, in your justice,
because of those who lie in wait;
make clear your way before me.

No truth can be found in their mouths,
their heart is all mischief,
their throat a wide-open grave,
all honey their speech.

All those you protect shall be glad
and ring out their joy.
You shelter them, in you they rejoice,
those who love your name.

It is you who bless the just man, Lord:
you surround him with favor as with a shield.

Glory to the Father, and to the Son, and to the Holy Spirit:
as it was in the beginning, is now, and will be for ever. Amen.

Psalm-prayer

Lord, all justice and all goodness come from you; you hate evil and abhor lies. Lead us, your servants, in the path of your justice, so that all who hope in you may rejoice with the Church and in Christ.

Psalm 29

A tribute of praise to the Word of God

The Father's voice proclaimed: "This is my beloved Son" (Matthew 3:17).

O GIVE the Lord, you sons of God,
give the Lord glory and power;
give the Lord the glory of his name.
Adore the Lord in his holy court.

The Lord's voice resounding on the waters,
the Lord on the immensity of waters;
the voice of the Lord, full of power,
the voice of the Lord, full of splendor.

The Lord's voice shattering the cedars,
the Lord shatters the cedars of Lebanon;
he makes Lebanon leap like a calf
and Sirion like a young wild-ox.

The Lord's voice flashes flames of fire.
The Lord's voice shaking the wilderness,
the Lord shakes the wilderness of Kadesh;
the Lord's voice rending the oak tree
and stripping the forest bare.

The God of glory thunders.
In his temple they all cry: "Glory!"
The Lord sat enthroned over the flood;
the Lord sits as king for ever.

The Lord will give strength to his people,
the Lord will bless his people with peace.

Glory to the Father, and to the Son, and to the Holy Spirit:
as it was in the beginning, is now, and will be for ever. Amen.

Psalm-prayer

You live for ever, Lord and King. All things of the earth justly sing your glory and honor. Strengthen your people against evil that we may rejoice in your peace and trust in your eternal promise.

Reading

2 Thessalonians 3:10b-13

WE gave you a rule when we were with you: not to let anyone have any food if he refused to do any work. Now we hear that there are some of you who are living in idleness, doing no work themselves but interfering with everyone else's. In the Lord Jesus Christ, we order and call on people of this kind to go on quietly working and earning the food that they eat.

My brothers, never grow tired of doing what is right.

Responsory

Blessed be the Lord our God,
blessed from age to age.
—Blessed be the Lord our God,
blessed from age to age.
His marvelous works are beyond compare,
—blessed from age to age.
Glory to the Father, and to the Son, and to the Holy Spirit.
—Blessed be the Lord our God,
blessed from age to age.

Antiphon

Blessed be the Lord our God.

Canticle of Zechariah

The Messiah and his forerunner

BLESSED be the Lord, the God of Israel;
he has come to his people and set them free.

He has raised up for us a mighty savior,
born of the house of his servant David.

Through his holy prophets he promised of old
that he would save us from our enemies,
from the hands of all who hate us.

He promised to show mercy to our fathers
and to remember his holy covenant.

This was the oath he swore to our father Abraham:
to set us free from the hands of our enemies,
free to worship him without fear,
holy and righteous in his sight
all the days of our life.

You, my child, shall be called the prophet of the Most High;
for you will go before the Lord to prepare his way,
to give his people knowledge of salvation
by the forgiveness of their sins.

In the tender compassion of our God
the dawn from on high shall break upon us,
to shine on those who dwell in darkness and the shadow of death,
and to guide our feet into the way of peace.

Glory to the Father, and to the Son, and to the Holy Spirit:
as it was in the beginning, is now, and will be for ever. Amen.

(For music, turn to p. 131)

Intercessions

WE ESTEEM Christ above all men, for he was filled with grace and the Holy Spirit.
In faith let us implore him:
Give us your Spirit, Lord.

Grant us a peaceful day,
—when evening comes we will praise you with joy and purity of heart.
Let your splendor rest upon us today,
—direct the work of our hands.
May your face shine upon us and keep us in peace,
—may your strong arm protect us.
Look kindly on all who put their trust in our prayers,
—fill them with every bodily and spiritual grace.

Our Father . . .

Prayer

FATHER,
may everything we do
begin with your inspiration
and continue with your saving help.
Let our work always find its origin in you
and through you reach completion.

We ask this through our Lord Jesus Christ, your Son,
who lives and reigns with you and the Holy Spirit,
God, for ever and ever.

(Dismissal, p. 133)

MONDAY EVENING

Reflection

THE voices speaking to the soul in the opening verses of Psalm 11 are voices we hear too: "Fly like a bird to its mountain."

Often as we look back in the evening over the uneven picture of our day, fear and discouragement speak to us like this: Flee!

You have done nothing today, they say. Nothing but hurt and disappointment, and still so much to do. Your ideals are unattainable; your hopes are misplaced. Give up, they say. Escape!

"In the Lord I have taken my refuge" (Ps 11).

The Lord, our refuge, does not tell us to escape from life however. He is a warrior who marches with those engaged in life's struggles. To draw on his strength we must continue in the battle, not retreat.

Psalm 15 lists basic guiding principles for involving ourselves in life. Justice, truthfulness and constancy are not easy to practice. They are the virtues of a warrior, and we who follow Christ must live them "to be holy and blameless in his sight."

"You will have in you the strength, based on his own glorious power, never to give in, but to bear anything joyfully . . ." (Colossians 1:11).

EVENING PRAYER

GOD, come to my assistance.
—Lord, make haste to help me.

Glory to the Father, and to the Son, and to the Holy Spirit:
—as it was in the beginning, is now, and will be for ever. Amen. Alleluia.

Antiphon

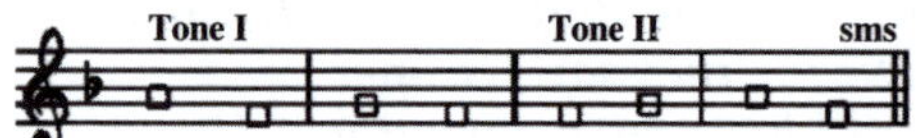

Psalm 11

God is the unfailing support of the just

Blessed are those who hunger and thirst for justice; they shall be satisfied (Matthew 5:6).

IN THE Lord I have taken my refuge.
How can you say to my soul:
"Fly like a bird to its mountain.

See the wicked bracing their bow;
they are fixing their arrows on the string
to shoot upright men in the dark.
Foundations once destroyed, what can the just do?"

The Lord is in his holy temple,
the Lord, whose throne is in heaven.
His eyes look down on the world;
his gaze tests mortal men.

The Lord tests the just and the wicked:
the lover of violence he hates.
He sends fire and brimstone on the wicked;
he sends a scorching wind as their lot.

The Lord is just and loves justice:
the upright shall see his face.

Glory to the Father, and to the Son, and to the Holy Spirit:
as it was in the beginning, is now, and will be for ever. Amen.

Psalm-prayer

Lord God, you search the hearts of all, both the good and the wicked. May those who are in danger for love of you, find security in you now, and, in the day of judgment, may they rejoice in seeing you face to face.

Antiphon

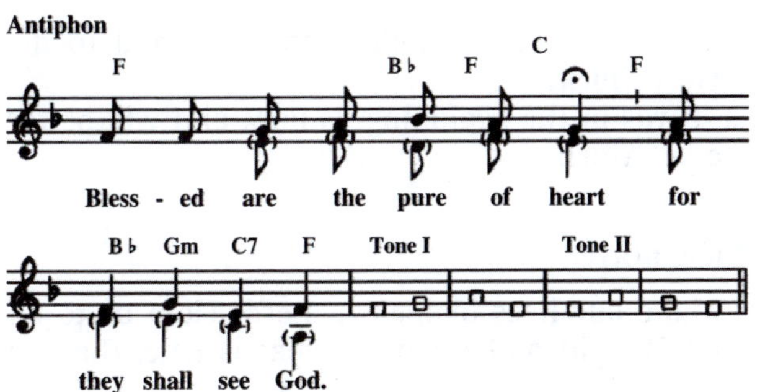

Psalm 15

Who is worthy to stand in God's presence?

You have come to Mount Zion, to the city of the living God (Hebrews 12:22).

LORD, who shall be admitted to your tent
and dwell on your holy mountain?

He who walks without fault;
he who acts with justice
and speaks the truth from his heart;
he who does not slander with his tongue;

he who does no wrong to his brother,
who casts no slur on his neighbor,
who holds the godless in disdain,
but honors those who fear the Lord;

he who keeps his pledge, come what may;
who takes no interest on a loan
accepts no bribes against the innocent.
Such a man will stand firm for ever.

Glory to the Father, and to the Son, and to the Holy Spirit:
as it was in the beginning, is now, and will be for ever. Amen.

Psalm-prayer

Make our lives blameless, Lord. Help us to do what is right and to speak what is true, that we may dwell in your tent and find rest on your holy mountain.

Reading

Colossians 1:9b-11

WHAT we ask God is that through perfect wisdom and spiritual understanding you should reach the fullest knowledge of his will. So you will be able to lead the kind of life which the Lord expects of you, a life acceptable to him in all its aspects; showing the results in all the good actions you do and increasing your knowledge of God. You will have in you the strength, based on his own glorious power, never to give in, but to bear anything joyfully.

Responsory

Lord, you alone can heal me, for I have grieved you by my sins.
—Lord, you alone can heal me, for I have grieved you by my sins.
Once more I say: O Lord, have mercy on me,
—for I have grieved you by my sins.
Glory to the Father, and to the Son, and to the Holy Spirit.
—Lord, you alone can heal me, for I have grieved you by my sins.

Antiphon

My soul proclaims the greatness of the Lord, for he has looked with favor on his lowly servant.

Canticle of Mary

The soul rejoices in the Lord

MY SOUL proclaims the greatness of the Lord,
my spirit rejoices in God my Savior
for he has looked with favor on his lowly servant.

From this day all generations will call me blessed:
the Almighty has done great things for me,
and holy is his Name.

He has mercy on those who fear him
in every generation.

He has shown the strength of his arm,
he has scattered the proud in their conceit.

He has cast down the mighty from their thrones,
and has lifted up the lowly.

He has filled the hungry with good things
and the rich he has sent away empty.

He has come to the help of his servant Israel
for he has remembered his promise of mercy,
the promise he made to our fathers,
to Abraham and his children for ever.

Glory to the Father, and to the Son, and to the Holy Spirit:
as it was in the beginning, is now, and will be for ever. Amen.

(For music, turn to p. 132)

Intercessions

GOD has made an everlasting covenant with his people, and he never ceases to bless them. Grateful for these gifts, we confidently direct our prayer to him:

Lord, bless your people.

Save your people, Lord,
—and bless your inheritance.

Gather into one body all who bear the name of Christian,
—that the world may believe in Christ whom you have sent.

Give our friends and our loved ones a share in divine life,
—let them be symbols of Christ before men.

Show your love to those who are suffering,
—open their eyes to the vision of your revelation.

Be compassionate to those who have died,
—welcome them into the company of the faithful departed.

Our Father . . .

Prayer

FATHER,
may this evening pledge of our service to you
bring you glory and praise.
For our salvation you looked with favor
on the lowliness of the Virgin Mary;

lead us to the fullness of the salvation
you have prepared for us.

We ask this through our Lord Jesus Christ, your Son,
who lives and reigns with you and the Holy Spirit,
God, for ever and ever.

(Dismissal, p. 133)

TUESDAY MORNING

Reflection

THE day is before us. God is within it already, waiting in creation and in the hours which will unfold before us according to the "plans of his heart" (Psalm 33:9). Yet, he also waits till we bring him to this day.

Psalm 24, a processional Psalm, celebrates these two themes. It is the song of the ancient Israelites as they carried the Ark of the Covenant into the Temple bearing the Lord with them in procession. We, too, bear God himself where we go today, and consequently the ground itself on which we walk must become holy. God is present in the world we enter today, yet he seeks human hearts and minds and actions to manifest his presence in a unique way. We cannot do this simply through physical living, however. Our hearts and desires are the great instruments that reveal him.

When we hear the cries of the Psalm, "O gates, lift high your heads. . . . Let him enter, the king of glory!" we need not think only of the gates of a special place. Perhaps we are asking that the gates of routine, of limited life, of sin be lifted; that what obstructs and diminishes our power to bring the Lord where we go may be removed, so that the "King of Glory" may be revealed.

The revelation of God in our lives becomes more difficult in our land of exile. Like Tobit, we must praise God in this difficult land "and manifest his power and majesty to a sinful nation" (Tobit 13:6).

Psalm 33 returns to the opening theme of Psalm 24. The Lord is already present in his creation and in the movement of history. Even the place of exile is in his power.

MORNING PRAYER

LORD, open my lips.
—And my mouth will proclaim your praise.
Glory to, etc.: —as it was, etc.

Antiphon

Come, let us worship our mighty King and Lord.

Invitatory psalm, p. 126.

Antiphon

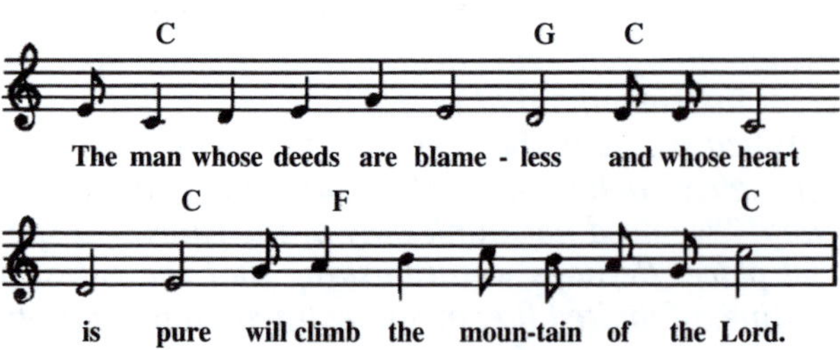

Psalm 24

The Lord's entry into his temple

Christ opened heaven for us in the manhood he assumed (Saint Irenaeus).

THE Lord's is the earth and its fullness,
the world and all its peoples.
It is he who set it on the seas;
on the waters he made it firm.

Who shall climb the mountain of the Lord?
Who shall stand in his holy place?
The man with clean hands and pure heart,
who desires not worthless things,
who has not sworn so as to deceive his neighbor.

He shall receive blessings from the Lord
and reward from the God who saves him.
Such are the men who seek him,
seek the face of the God of Jacob.

O gates, lift high your heads;
grow higher, ancient doors.
Let him enter, the king of glory!

Who is the king of glory?
The Lord, the mighty, the valiant,
the Lord, the valiant in war.

O gates, lift high your heads;
grow higher, ancient doors.
Let him enter, the king of glory!

Who is he, the king of glory?
He, the Lord of armies,
he is the king of glory.

Glory to the Father, and to the Son, and to the Holy Spirit:
as it was in the beginning, is now, and will be for ever. Amen.

Psalm-prayer

King of glory, Lord of power and might, cleanse our hearts from all sin, preserve the innocence of our hands, and keep our minds from vanity, so that we may deserve your blessing in your holy place.

Psalm 33

Song of praise for God's continual care

Through the Word all things were made (John 1:3).

RING out your joy to the Lord, O you just;
for praise is fitting for loyal hearts.

Give thanks to the Lord upon the harp,
with a ten-stringed lute sing him songs.
O sing him a song that is new,
play loudly, with all your skill.

For the word of the Lord is faithful
and all his works to be trusted.

The Lord loves justice and right
and fills the earth with his love.

By his word the heavens were made,
by the breath of his mouth all the stars.
He collects the waves of the ocean;
he stores up the depths of the sea.

Let all the earth fear the Lord,
all who live in the world revere him.
He spoke; and it came to be.
He commanded; it sprang into being.

He frustrates the designs of the nations,
he defeats the plans of the peoples.
His own designs shall stand for ever,
the plans of his heart from age to age.

They are happy, whose God is the Lord,
the people he has chosen as his own.
From the heavens the Lord looks forth,
he sees all the children of men.

From the place where he dwells he gazes
on all the dwellers on the earth,
he who shapes the hearts of them all
and considers all their deeds.

A king is not saved by his army,
nor a warrior preserved by his strength.
A vain hope for safety is the horse;
despite its power it cannot save.

The Lord looks on those who revere him,
on those who hope in his love,
to rescue their souls from death,
to keep them alive in famine.

Our soul is waiting for the Lord.
The Lord is our help and our shield.
In him do our hearts find joy.
We trust in his holy name.

May your love be upon us, O Lord,
as we place all our hope in you.

Glory to the Father, and to the Son, and to the Holy Spirit:
as it was in the beginning, is now, and will be for ever. Amen.

Psalm-prayer

Nourish your people, Lord, for we hunger for your word. Rescue us from the death of sin and fill us with your mercy, that we may share your presence and the joys of all the saints.

Reading

Romans 13:11b, 12-13a

YOU must wake up now. The night is almost over, it will be daylight soon—let us give up all the things we prefer to do under cover of the dark; let us arm ourselves and appear in the light. Let us live decently as people do in the daytime.

Responsory

My God stands by me, all my trust is in him.
—My God stands by me, all my trust is in him.
I find refuge in him, and I am truly free.
—all my trust is in him.

Glory to the Father, and to the Son, and to the Holy Spirit.
—My God stands by me, all my trust is in him.

Antiphon

God has raised up for us a mighty Savior, as he promised through the words of his holy prophets.

Canticle of Zechariah

The Messiah and his forerunner

BLESSED be the Lord, the God of Israel;
he has come to his people and set them free.

He has raised up for us a mighty savior,
born of the house of his servant David.

Through his holy prophets he promised of old
that he would save us from our enemies,
from the hands of all who hate us.

He promised to show mercy to our fathers
and to remember his holy covenant.

This was the oath he swore to our father Abraham:
to set us free from the hands of our enemies,
free to worship him without fear,
holy and righteous in his sight
all the days of our life.

You, my child, shall be called the prophet of the Most High;
for you will go before the Lord to prepare his way,

to give his people knowledge of salvation
by the forgiveness of their sins.

In the tender compassion of our God
the dawn from on high shall break upon us,
to shine on those who dwell in darkness and the shadow of death,
and to guide our feet into the way of peace.

Glory to the Father, and to the Son, and to the Holy Spirit:
as it was in the beginning, is now, and will be for ever. Amen.

(For music, turn to p. 131)

Intercessions

BELOVED brothers and sisters, we share a heavenly calling under Christ, our high priest. Let us praise him with shouts of joy:
Lord, our God and our Savior.

Almighty King, through baptism you conferred on us a royal priesthood,
—inspire us to offer you a continual sacrifice of praise.

Help us to keep your commandments,
—that through the power of the Holy Spirit we may live in you and you in us.

Give us your eternal wisdom,
—to be with us today and to guide us.

May our companions today be free of sorrow,
—and filled with joy.

Our Father . . .

Prayer

**GOD our Father,
hear our morning prayer
and let the radiance of your love
scatter the gloom of our hearts.
The light of heaven's love has restored us to life:
free us from the desires that belong to darkness.**

**We ask this through our Lord Jesus Christ, your Son,
who lives and reigns with you and the Holy Spirit,
God, for ever and ever.**

(Dismissal, p. 133)

TUESDAY EVENING

Reflection

TWO royal Psalms begin this evening's prayer. Psalm 20 is an ancient Jewish prayer asking that the king be victorious in battle. Psalm 21 is a prayer of thanksgiving for a victory the king has achieved.

Both these Psalms reveal the strong bond between the Israelites and their king. As God's anointed, the king lifted the spirits of his people and gave them hope. He was the rallying point of the nation, which shared his cause and achievements.

As Christians, we relate this way to Christ, whose life and destiny commingle with ours. The passion of Christ, his great battle, still goes on in us, the Body of Christ on earth. Similarly, we share in his Resurrection and victory. In these two royal Psalms, therefore, we pray in solidarity with Christ, our King.

The first Letter of John, too, proclaims our present and future union in Jesus Christ. What that union will bring we have yet to see. God has promised that "we shall be like him . . . as he is" (1 John 3:2)—"a kingdom and priests to serve our God" (Revelation 5:10), sharing the power and glory of Christ.

Our lives are not small and insignificant. We are not isolated and alone. The Psalms, reading, and prayers for this evening remind us of the dignity and destiny we share with Christ, our Lord.

EVENING PRAYER

GOD, come to my assistance.
—Lord, make haste to help me.

Glory to the Father, and to the Son, and to the Holy Spirit:
—as it was in the beginning, is now, and will be for ever. Amen. Alleluia.

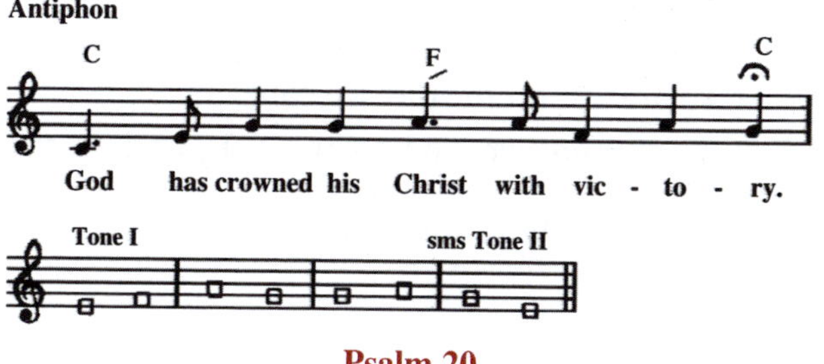

Psalm 20

A prayer for the king's victory

Whoever calls upon the name of the Lord will be saved (Acts 2:21).

MAY the Lord answer in time of trial;
may the name of Jacob's God protect you.

May he send you help from his shrine
and give you support from Zion.
May he remember all your offerings
and receive your sacrifice with favor.

May he give you your heart's desire
and fulfill every one of your plans.

May we ring out our joy at your victory
and rejoice in the name of our God.
May the Lord grant all your prayers.

I am sure now that the Lord
will give victory to his anointed,
will reply from his holy heaven
with the mighty victory of his hand.

Some trust in chariots or horses,
but we in the name of the Lord.
They will collapse and fall,
but we shall hold and stand firm.

Give victory to the king, O Lord,
give answer on the day we call.

Glory to the Father, and to the Son, and to the Holy Spirit:
as it was in the beginning, is now, and will be for ever. Amen.

Psalm-prayer

Lord, you accepted the perfect sacrifice of your Son upon the cross. Hear us during times of trouble and protect us by the power of his name, that we who share his struggle on earth may merit a share in his victory.

Psalm 21:2-8, 14

Thanksgiving for the king's victory

He accepted life that he might rise and live for ever (Saint Hilary).

O LORD, your strength gives joy to the king;
how your saving help makes him glad!
You have granted him his heart's desire;
you have not refused the prayer of his lips.

You came to meet him with the blessings of success,
you have set on his head a crown of pure gold.
He asked you for life and this you have given,
days that will last from age to age.

Your saving help has given him glory.
You have laid upon him majesty and splendor,
you have granted your blessings to him for ever.
You have made him rejoice with the joy of your presence.

The king has put his trust in the Lord:
through the mercy of the Most High he shall stand firm.
O Lord, arise in your strength;
we shall sing and praise your power.

Glory to the Father, and to the Son, and to the Holy Spirit:
as it was in the beginning, is now, and will be for ever. Amen.

Psalm-prayer

Father, you have given us life on this earth and have met us with the grace of redemption. Bestow your greatest blessing on us, the fullness of eternal life.

Reading

1 John 3:1a, 2

THINK of the love that the Father has lavished on us,
by letting us be called God's children;
and that is what we are.
My dear people, we are already the children of God
but what we are to be in the future has not yet been revealed;
all we know is, that when it is revealed
we shall be like him
because we shall see him as he really is.

Responsory

Through all eternity, O Lord, your promise stands unshaken.
—Through all eternity, O Lord, your promise stands unshaken.
Your faithfulness will never fail;
—your promise stands unshaken.
Glory to the Father, and to the Son, and to the Holy Spirit.
—Through all eternity, O Lord, your promise stands unshaken.

Antiphon

My spirit rejoices in God my Savior.

Canticle of Mary

The soul rejoices in the Lord

MY SOUL proclaims the greatness of the Lord,
my spirit rejoices in God my Savior
for he has looked with favor on his lowly servant.

From this day all generations will call me blessed:
the Almighty has done great things for me,
and holy is his Name.

He has mercy on those who fear him
in every generation.

He has shown the strength of his arm,
he has scattered the proud in their conceit.

He has cast down the mighty from their thrones,
and has lifted up the lowly.

He has filled the hungry with good things
and the rich he has sent away empty.

He has come to the help of his servant Israel
for he has remembered his promise of mercy,
the promise he made to our fathers,
to Abraham and his children for ever.

Glory to the Father, and to the Son, and to the Holy Spirit:
as it was in the beginning, is now, and will be for ever. Amen.

(For music, turn to p. 132)

Intercessions

LET us praise Christ the Lord, who lives among us, the people he redeemed, and let us say:
Lord, hear our prayer.

Lord, king and ruler of nations, be with all your people and their governments,
—inspire them to pursue the good of all according to your law.

You made captive our captivity,
—to our brothers who are enduring bodily or spiritual chains, grant the freedom of the sons of God.

May our young people be concerned with remaining blameless in your sight,
—and may they generously follow your call.

May our children imitate your example,
—and grow in wisdom and grace.

Accept our dead brothers and sisters into your eternal kingdom,
—where we hope to reign with you.

Our Father . . .

Prayer

ALMIGHTY God,
we give you thanks
for bringing us safely
to this evening hour.
May this lifting up of our hands in prayer
be a sacrifice pleasing in your sight.

We ask this through our Lord Jesus Christ, your Son
who lives . . . for ever and ever. (Dismissal, p. 133)

WEDNESDAY MORNING

Reflection

PSALM 36 begins this morning's prayer cautioning us to beware of sin.

"Sin speaks to the sinner in the depths of his heart."

Sin and evil cast their dark spell everywhere, but their favorite home is the human heart. There they foster self-deception, hostility toward others and forgetfulness of God. The sinner within us knows how enticing the call of wickedness is.

God's goodness, however, is stronger no matter how powerful sin may appear. The light of his grace brightens the heights and the depths, overcoming all darkness.

The story of Judith, the Jewess who killed the powerful oppressive king, Holofernes, reveals the way God's mercy overturns evil. Using the frailest and weakest of his people—but one who depended on him—God destroyed a stronghold of sin. The song of Judith (16:2-3a, 13-15) is the song of one who triumphed over invincible odds because she hoped in the Lord.

We should be aware of sin as we go on our way today. But, more importantly, we should rejoice in God's strong grace, which is given to us.

Psalm 47 further celebrates God's mighty power present in Jesus Christ, the King of all nations.

MORNING PRAYER

LORD, open my lips.
—And my mouth will proclaim your praise.
Glory to, etc.: —as it was, etc.

Antiphon

Come, let us worship before the Lord, our maker.

Invitatory psalm, p. 126.

Antiphon

Psalm 36

The malice of sinners and God's goodness

***No follower of mine wanders in the dark; he shall have the light of life* (John 8:12).**

SIN speaks to the sinner
in the depths of his heart.
There is no fear of God
before his eyes.

He so flatters himself in his mind
that he knows not his guilt.
In his mouth are mischief and deceit.
All wisdom is gone.

He so flatters himself in his mind
as he lies on his bed.
He has set his foot on evil ways,
he clings to what is evil.

Your love, Lord, reaches to heaven;
your truth to the skies.
Your justice is like God's mountain,
your judgments like the deep.

To both man and beast you give protection.
O Lord, how precious is your love.
My God, the sons of men
find refuge in the shelter of your wings.

They feast on the riches of your house;
they drink from the stream of your delight.
In you is the source of life
and in your light we see light.

Keep on loving those who know you,
doing justice for upright hearts.
Let the foot of the proud not crush me
nor the hand of the wicked cast me out.

See how the evil-doers fall!
Flung down, they shall never rise.

Glory to the Father, and to the Son, and to the Holy Spirit:
as it was in the beginning, is now, and will be for ever. Amen.

Psalm-prayer

Lord, you are the source of unfailing light. Give us true knowledge of your mercy so that we may renounce our pride and be filled with the riches of your house.

Antiphon

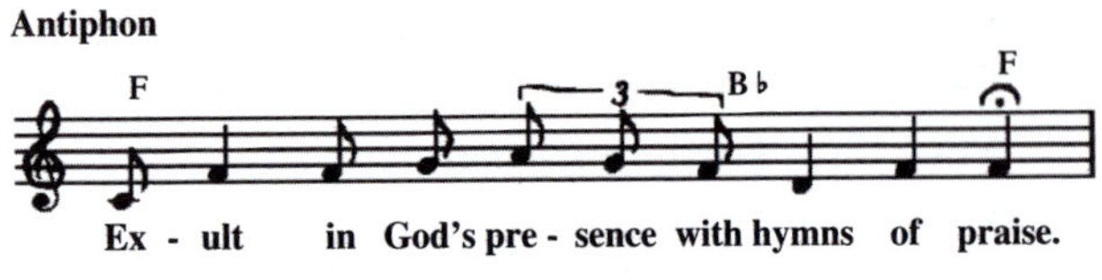

Psalm 47

The Lord Jesus is King of all

He is seated at the right hand of the Father, and his kingdom will have no end.

ALL peoples, clap your hands,
cry to God with shouts of joy!
For the Lord, the Most High, we must fear,
great king over all the earth.

He subdues peoples under us
and nations under our feet.
Our inheritance, our glory, is from him,
given to Jacob out of love.

God goes up with shouts of joy;
the Lord goes up with trumpet blast.
Sing praise for God, sing praise,
sing praise to our king, sing praise.

God is king of all the earth.
Sing praise with all your skill.
God is king over the nations;
God reigns on his holy throne.

The princes of the peoples are assembled
with the people of Abraham's God.
The rulers of the earth belong to God,
to God who reigns over all.

Glory to the Father, and to the Son, and to the Holy Spirit:
as it was in the beginning, is now, and will be for ever. Amen.

Psalm-prayer

God, King of all peoples and all ages, it is your victory we celebrate as we sing with all the skill at our command. Help us always to overcome evil by good, that we may rejoice in your triumph for ever.

Reading

Tobit 4:15a, 16a, 18a, 19

DO TO no one what you would not want done to you. Give your bread to those who are hungry, and your clothes to those who are naked. Ask advice of every wise person. Bless the Lord God in everything; beg him to guide your ways and bring your paths and purposes to their end.

Responsory

Incline my heart according to your will, O God.
—Incline my heart according to your will, O God.

Speed my steps along your path,
—according to your will, O God.
Glory to the Father, and to the Son, and to the Holy Spirit.
—Incline my heart according to your will, O God.

Antiphon

Show us your mercy, Lord; remember your holy covenant.

Canticle of Zechariah

The Messiah and his forerunner

BLESSED be the Lord, the God of Israel;
he has come to his people and set them free.

He has raised up for us a mighty savior,
born of the house of his servant David.

Through his holy prophets he promised of old
that he would save us from our enemies,
from the hands of all who hate us.

He promised to show mercy to our fathers
and to remember his holy covenant.

This was the oath he swore to our father Abraham:
to set us free from the hands of our enemies,
free to worship him without fear,
holy and righteous in his sight
all the days of our life.

You, my child, shall be called the prophet of the Most High;

for you will go before the Lord to prepare his way,
to give his people knowledge of salvation
by the forgiveness of their sins.

In the tender compassion of our God
the dawn from on high shall break upon us,
to shine on those who dwell in darkness and the shadow of death,
and to guide our feet into the way of peace.

Glory to the Father, and to the Son, and to the Holy Spirit:
as it was in the beginning, is now, and will be for ever. Amen.

(For music, turn to p. 131)

Intercessions

LET us give thanks to Christ and offer him continued praise, for he sanctifies us and calls us his brothers:

Lord, help your brothers to grow in holiness.

With single-minded devotion we dedicate the beginnings of this day to the honor of your Resurrection,
—may we make the whole day pleasing to you by our works of holiness.

As a sign of your love, you renew each day for the sake of our well-being and happiness,
—renew us daily for the sake of your glory.

Teach us today to recognize your presence in all men,
—especially in the poor and in those who mourn.

Grant that we may live today in peace with all men,
—never rendering evil for evil.

Our Father . . .

Prayer

GOD our Savior,
hear our morning prayer:
help us to follow the light
and live the truth.
In you we have been born again
as sons and daughters of light:
may we be your witnesses before all the world.

We ask this through our Lord Jesus Christ, your Son,
who lives and reigns with you and the Holy Spirit,
God, for ever and ever.

(Dismissal, p. 133)

WEDNESDAY EVENING

Reflection

NO ONE ends a day without some scars. Count them within yourself. The day inflicts its wounds, sometimes painful indeed. Any account of twenty-four hours must list our experiences of hostility and misunderstanding from the world around us, as well as of conflict within.

Then, too, what has been accomplished? Time has passed. Yet have we done anything significant? Perhaps the psalmist in Psalm 27 is speaking to God from sentiments like these, seeking comfort and steadying from him in the wearying experience of life.

The psalmist enters the temple to be refreshed by the loveliness of the Lord, to feel the security of resting in God, the Rock. Our place of refreshment is Christ, the living temple. "Come to me, all you who are weary and overburdened and I will give you rest" (Matthew 11:28).

The saints in their trials found shelter in the Passion of Christ. "Where can our frailty find rest and security if not in the wounds of Christ?" St. Bernard asks. In Christ, who suffered and died,

God has become a compassionate companion to suffering humanity.

Psalm 27 ends with God's own strong words: "Hope in him, hold firm and take heart. Hope in the Lord!" The basis for our hope is Christ (cf Colossians 1:11-20): God has called us to his kingdom through Christ who redeemed us.

EVENING PRAYER

GOD, come to my assistance.
—Lord, make haste to help me.
Glory to the Father, and to the Son, and to the Holy Spirit:
—as it was in the beginning, is now, and will be for ever. Amen. Alleluia.

Antiphon

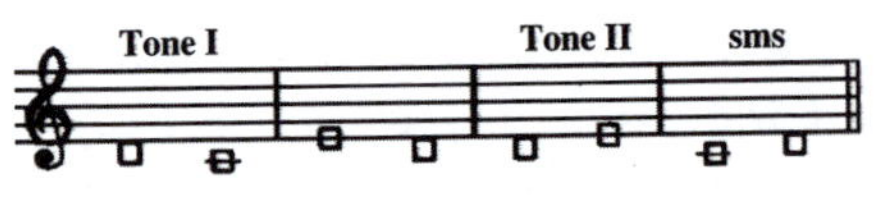

Psalm 27

God stands by us in dangers

God now truly dwells with men (Revelation 21:3).

I

THE Lord is my light and my help;
whom shall I fear?

The Lord is the stronghold of my life;
before whom shall I shrink?

When evil-doers draw near
to devour my flesh,
it is they, my enemies and foes,
who stumble and fall.

Though an army encamp against me
my heart would not fear.
Though war break out against me
even then would I trust.

There is one thing I ask of the Lord,
for this I long,
to live in the house of the Lord,
all the days of my life,
to savor the sweetness of the Lord,
to behold his temple.

For there he keeps me safe in his tent
in the day of evil.
He hides me in the shelter of his tent,
on a rock he sets me safe.

And now my head shall be raised
above my foes who surround me
and I shall offer within his tent
a sacrifice of joy.

I will sing and make music for the Lord.

Glory to the Father, and to the Son, and to the Holy Spirit:
as it was in the beginning, is now, and will be for ever. Amen.

II

O LORD, hear my voice when I call;
have mercy and answer.
Of you my heart has spoken:
"Seek his face."

It is your face, O Lord, that I seek;
hide not your face.
Dismiss not your servant in anger;
you have been my help.

Do not abandon or forsake me,
O God my help!
Though father and mother forsake me,
the Lord will receive me.

Instruct me, Lord, in your way;
on an even path lead me.
When they lie in ambush protect me
from my enemy's greed.
False witnesses rise against me,
breathing out fury.

I am sure I shall see the Lord's goodness
in the land of the living.

Hope in him, hold firm and take heart.
Hope in the Lord!

Glory to the Father, and to the Son, and to the Holy Spirit:
as it was in the beginning, is now, and will be for ever. Amen.

Psalm-prayer

Father, you protect and strengthen those who hope in you; you heard the cry of your Son and kept him safe in your tent in the day of evil. Grant that your servants who seek your face in times of trouble may see your goodness in the land of the living.

Reading

James 1:22, 25

YOU must do what the word tells you, and not just listen to it and deceive yourselves. The man who looks steadily at the perfect law of freedom and makes that his habit—not listening and then forgetting, but actively putting it into practice—will be happy in all that he does.

Responsory

Claim me once more as your own, Lord, and have mercy on me.
—Claim me once more as your own, Lord, and have mercy on me.
Do not abandon me with the wicked;
—have mercy on me.

Glory to the Father, and to the Son, and to the Holy Spirit.
—Claim me once more as your own, Lord, and have mercy on me.

Antiphon

The Almighty has done great things for me, and holy is his Name.

Canticle of Mary

The soul rejoices in the Lord

MY SOUL proclaims the greatness of the Lord,
my spirit rejoices in God my Savior
for he has looked with favor on his lowly servant.

From this day all generations will call me blessed:
the Almighty has done great things for me,
and holy is his Name.

He has mercy on those who fear him
in every generation.

He has shown the strength of his arm,
he has scattered the proud in their conceit.

He has cast down the mighty from their thrones,
and has lifted up the lowly.

He has filled the hungry with good things
and the rich he has sent away empty.

He has come to the help of his servant Israel
for he has remembered his promise of mercy,
the promise he made to our fathers,
to Abraham and his children for ever.

Glory to the Father, and to the Son, and to the Holy Spirit:
as it was in the beginning, is now, and will be for ever. Amen.

(For music, turn to p. 132)

Intercessions

IN ALL we do, let the name of the Lord be praised, for he surrounds his chosen people with boundless love. Let our prayer rise up to him:
Lord, show us your love.

Remember your Church, Lord,
—keep her from every evil and let her grow to the fullness of your love.

Let the nations recognize you as the one true God,
—and Jesus your Son, as the Messiah whom you sent.

Grant prosperity to our neighbors,
—give them life and happiness for ever.

Console those who are burdened with oppressive work and daily hardships,
—preserve the dignity of workers.

Open wide the doors of your compassion to those who have died today,
—and in your mercy receive them into your kingdom.

Our Father . . .

Prayer

LORD,
watch over us by day and by night.
In the midst of life's countless changes
strengthen us with your never-changing love.

We ask this through our Lord Jesus Christ, your Son,
who lives and reigns with you and the Holy Spirit,
God, for ever and ever.

(Dismissal, p. 133)

THURSDAY MORNING

Reflection

SAINT Augustine calls Psalm 57, the first Psalm for this morning's prayer, a prayer of Jesus Christ in his passion. It is our prayer, too, as members of Christ. "The whole Christ is speaking here; here is your voice too."

Whatever conflict and suffering this day brings, we are prepared to meet it in Christ. "My heart is ready, O God."

The weak, the poor in spirit, the sinner, gathered together by God's redeeming love, will make the journey to his kingdom. Poor as we are, we can rely on God's promise of strength for this day's journey.

The final Psalm, 48, celebrates God's saving presence in Zion, his holy city. This is a favorite theme in the Psalms.

God is indeed everywhere, but he is especially present in his people and his church.

Praise and appreciate God's gifts in those around you, this Psalm proclaims. Recognize God's presence in those who are nearest you. Don't miss his power in what is closest to you.

Walk through Zion, walk all round it;
count the number of its towers.
Review all its ramparts,
examine its castles.

MORNING PRAYER

LORD open my lips.
—And my mouth will proclaim your praise.
Glory to, etc.: —as it was, etc.

Antiphon

Come, let us worship the Lord, for he is our God.

Invitatory psalm, p 126.

Antiphon

Psalm 57

Morning prayer in affliction

This psalm tells of our Lord's passion (Saint Augustine).

HAVE mercy on me, God, have mercy
for in you my soul has taken refuge.
In the shadow of your wings I take refuge
till the storms of destruction pass by.

I call to God the Most High,
to God who has always been my help.
May he send from heaven and save me
and shame those who assail me.

May God send his truth and his love.
My soul lies down among lions,
who would devour the sons of men.
Their teeth are spears and arrows,
their tongue a sharpened sword.

O God, arise above the heavens;
may your glory shine on earth!

They laid a snare for my steps,
my soul was bowed down.
They dug a pit in my path
but fell in it themselves.

My heart is ready, O God,
my heart is ready.
I will sing, I will sing your praise.
Awake, my soul,
awake, lyre and harp,
I will awake the dawn.

I will thank you, Lord, among the peoples,
among the nations I will praise you
for your love reaches to the heavens
and your truth to the skies.

O God, arise above the heavens;
may your glory shine on earth!

Glory to the Father, and to the Son, and to the Holy Spirit:
as it was in the beginning, is now, and will be for ever. Amen.

Psalm-prayer

Lord, send your mercy and your truth to rescue us from the snares of the devil, and we will praise you among the peoples and proclaim you to the nations, happy to be known as companions of your Son.

Antiphon

Psalm 48

Thanksgiving for the people's deliverance

He took me up a high mountain and showed me Jerusalem, God's holy city (Revelation 21:10).

THE Lord is great and worthy to be praised
in the city of our God.
His holy mountain rises in beauty,
the joy of all the earth.

Mount Zion, true pole of the earth,
the Great King's city!
God, in the midst of its citadels,
has shown himself its stronghold.

For the kings assembled together,
together they advanced.
They saw; at once they were astounded;
dismayed, they fled in fear.

A trembling seized them there,
like the pangs of birth.

By the east wind you have destroyed
the ships of Tarshish.

As we have heard, so we have seen
in the city of our God,
in the city of the Lord of hosts
which God upholds for ever.

O God, we ponder your love
within your temple.
Your praise, O God, like your name
reaches to the ends of the earth.

With justice your right hand is filled.
Mount Zion rejoices;
the people of Judah rejoice
at the sight of your judgments.

Walk through Zion, walk all round it;
count the number of its towers.
Review all its ramparts,
examine its castles,

that you may tell the next generation
that such is our God,
our God for ever and always.
It is he who leads us.

Glory to the Father, and to the Son, and to the Holy Spirit:
as it was in the beginning, is now, and will be for ever. Amen.

Psalm-prayer

Father, the body of your risen Son is the temple not made by human hands and the defending wall of the new Jerusalem. May this holy city, built of living stones, shine with spiritual radiance and witness to your greatness in the sight of all nations.

Reading

Isaiah 66:1-2

THUS says Yahweh:
With heaven my throne
and earth my footstool,
what house could you build me,
what place could you make for my rest?
All of this was made by my hand and all of this is mine—it is Yahweh who speaks.
But my eyes are drawn to the man of humbled and contrite spirit,
who trembles at my word.

Responsory

From the depths of my heart I cry to you: hear me, O Lord.
—From the depths of my heart I cry to you: hear me, O Lord.
I will do what you desire;
—hear me, O Lord.
Glory to the Father, and to the Son, and to the Holy Spirit.
—From the depths of my heart I cry to you: hear me, O Lord.

Antiphon

Let us serve the Lord in holiness, and he will save us from our enemies.

Canticle of Zechariah

The Messiah and his forerunner

BLESSED be the Lord, the God of Israel;
he has come to his people and set them free.

He has raised up for us a mighty savior,
born of the house of his servant David.

Through his holy prophets he promised of old
that he would save us from our enemies,
from the hands of all who hate us.

He promised to show mercy to our fathers
and to remember his holy covenant.

This was the oath he swore to our father Abraham:
to set us free from the hands of our enemies,
free to worship him without fear,
holy and righteous in his sight
all the days of our life.

You, my child, shall be called the prophet of the Most High;
for you will go before the Lord to prepare his way,
to give his people knowledge of salvation
by the forgiveness of their sins.

In the tender compassion of our God
the dawn from on high shall break upon us,
to shine on those who dwell in darkness and the shadow of death,
and to guide our feet into the way of peace.

Glory to the Father, and to the Son, and to the Holy Spirit:
as it was in the beginning, is now, and will be for ever. Amen.

(For music, turn to p. 131)

Intercessions

THE Lord Jesus Christ has given us the light of another day. In return we thank him as we cry out:

Lord, bless us and bring us close to you.

You offered yourself in sacrifice for our sins,
—accept our intentions and our work today.
You bring us joy by the light of another day,
—let the morning star rise in our hearts.
Give us strength to be patient with those we meet today,
—and so imitate you.
Make us aware of your mercy this morning, Lord,
—and let your strength be our delight.

Our Father . . .

Prayer

ALL-POWERFUL and ever-living God,
at morning, noon, and evening we pray:
cast out from our hearts the darkness of sin
and bring us to the light of your truth,
Jesus Christ, who lives and reigns with you and the Holy Spirit,
God, for ever and ever. (Dismissal, p. 133)

THURSDAY EVENING

Reflection

WE CELEBRATE evening prayer, says St. Basil, to "give thanks for what has been given us, or what we have done well during the day." Blessings too numerous to mention call for our acknowledgment.

One of God's greatest blessings is the hope of eternal life we have in Jesus Christ, who promised that those who believe in him "even if they die, shall live."

Night's coming warns us of the coming of her sister, Death. The end of all our mortal days is foreshadowed in the end of this one.

With Christ we look for life beyond the grave, however, where mourning will be changed into dancing and sorrow into joy (Psalm 30).

Even sin, the death of the soul, can be forgiven and new life imparted by God, if we but seek his forgiveness.

I will confess
my offense to the Lord.
And you, Lord, have forgiven
the guilt of my sin. (Psalm 32)

EVENING PRAYER

GOD, come to my assistance.
—Lord, make haste to help me.
Glory to the Father, and to the Son, and to the Holy Spirit:
—as it was in the beginning, is now, and will be for ever. Amen. Alleluia.

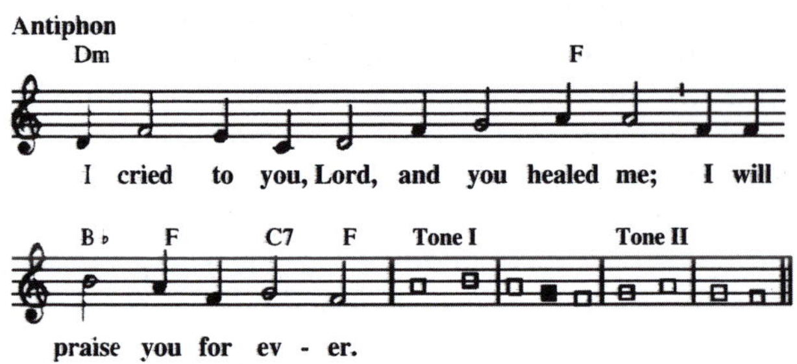

Psalm 30

Thanksgiving for deliverance from death

Christ, risen in glory, gives continual thanks to his Father (Cassian).

I WILL praise you, Lord, you have rescued me
and have not let my enemies rejoice over me.

O Lord, I cried to you for help
and you, my God, have healed me.
O Lord, you have raised my soul from the dead,
restored me to life from those who sink into the grave.

Sing psalms to the Lord, you who love him,
give thanks to his holy name.
His anger lasts a moment; his favor through life.
At night there are tears, but joy comes with dawn.

I said to myself in my good fortune:
"Nothing will ever disturb me."
Your favor had set me on a mountain fastness,
then you hid your face and I was put to confusion.

To you, Lord, I cried,
to my God I made appeal:
"What profit would my death be, my going to the grave?
Can dust give you praise or proclaim your truth?"

The Lord listened and had pity.
The Lord came to my help.
For me you have changed my mourning into dancing,
you removed my sackcloth and clothed me with joy.
So my soul sings psalms to you unceasingly.
O Lord my God, I will thank you for ever.

Glory to the Father, and to the Son, and to the Holy Spirit:
as it was in the beginning, is now, and will be for ever. Amen.

Psalm-prayer

God our Father, glorious in giving life, and even more glorious in restoring it, when his last night on earth came, your Son shed tears of blood, but dawn brought incomparable gladness. Do not turn away from us, or we shall fall back into dust, but rather turn our mourning into joy by raising us up with Christ.

Antiphon

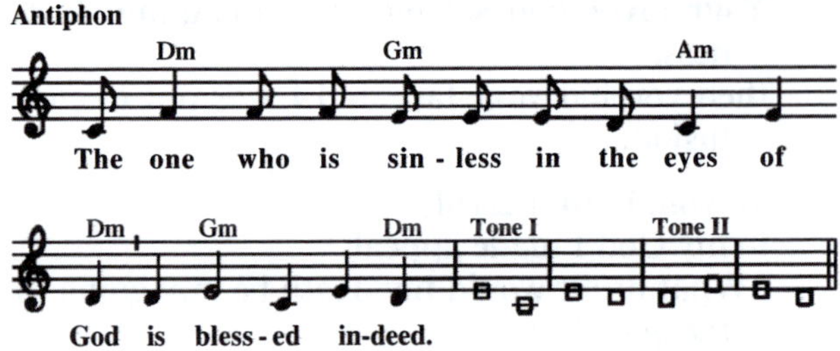

Psalm 32

They are happy whose sins are forgiven

David speaks of the happiness of the man who is holy in God's eyes not because of his own worth, but because God has justified him (Romans 4:6).

HAPPY the man whose offense is forgiven,
whose sin is remitted.
O happy the man to whom the Lord
imputes no guilt,
in whose spirit is no guile.

I kept it secret and my frame was wasted.
I groaned all the day long
for night and day your hand

was heavy upon me.
Indeed, my strength was dried up
as by the summer's heat.

But now I have acknowledged my sins;
my guilt I did not hide.
I said: "I will confess
my offense to the Lord."
And you, Lord, have forgiven
the guilt of my sin.

So let every good man pray to you
in the time of need.
The floods of water may reach high
but him they shall not reach.
You are my hiding place, O Lord;
you save me from distress.
You surround me with cries of deliverance.

I will instruct you and teach you
the way you should go;
I will give you counsel
with my eye upon you.

Be not like horse and mule, unintelligent,
needing bridle and bit,
else they will not approach you.
Many sorrows has the wicked
but he who trusts in the Lord,
loving mercy surrounds him.

Rejoice, rejoice in the Lord,
exult, you just!
O come, ring out your joy,
all you upright of heart.

Glory to the Father, and to the Son, and to the Holy Spirit:

as it was in the beginning, is now, and will be for ever. Amen.

Psalm-prayer

You desired, Lord, to keep from us your indignation and so did not spare Jesus Christ, who was wounded for our sins. We are your prodigal children, but confessing our sins we come back to you. Embrace us that we may rejoice in your mercy together with Christ your beloved Son.

Reading

1 Peter 1: 6-9

THIS is a cause of great joy for you, even though you may for a short time have to bear being plagued by all sorts of trials; so that, when Jesus Christ is revealed, your faith will have been tested and proved like gold—only it is more precious than gold, which is corruptible even though it bears testing by fire—and then you will have praise and glory and honor. You did not see him, yet you love him; and still without seeing him, you are already filled with a joy so glorious that it cannot be described, because you believe; and you are sure of the end to which your faith looks forward, that is, the salvation of your souls.

Responsory

The Lord has given us food, bread of the finest wheat.
—The Lord has given us food, bread of the finest wheat.

Honey from the rock to our heart's content,
—bread of the finest wheat.
Glory to the Father, and to the Son, and to the Holy Spirit.
—The Lord has given us food, bread of the finest wheat.

Antiphon

God has cast down the mighty from their thrones, and has lifted up the lowly.

Canticle of Mary

The soul rejoices in the Lord

MY SOUL proclaims the greatness of the Lord,
my spirit rejoices in God my Savior
for he has looked with favor on his lowly servant.

From this day all generations will call me blessed:
the Almighty has done great things for me,
and holy is his Name.

He has mercy on those who fear him
in every generation.

He has shown the strength of his arm,
he has scattered the proud in their conceit.

He has cast down the mighty from their thrones,
and has lifted up the lowly.

He has filled the hungry with good things
and the rich he has sent away empty.

He has come to the help of his servant Israel
for he has remembered his promise of mercy,
the promise he made to our fathers,
to Abraham and his children for ever.

Glory to the Father, and to the Son, and to the Holy Spirit:
as it was in the beginning, is now, and will be for ever. Amen.

(For music, turn to p. 132)

Intercessions

OUR hope is in God, who gives us help. Let us call upon him, and say:
Look kindly on your children, Lord.

Lord, our God, you made an eternal covenant with your people,
—keep us ever mindful of your mighty deeds.

Let your ordained ministers grow toward perfect love,
—and preserve your faithful people in unity by the bond of peace.

Be with us in our work of building the earthly city,
—that in building we may not labor in vain.

Send workers into your vineyard,
—and glorify your name among the nations.

Welcome into the company of your saints our relatives and benefactors who have died,
—may we share their happiness one day.

Our Father . . .

Prayer

FATHER,
you illumine the night
and bring the dawn to scatter darkness.
Let us pass this night in safety,
free from Satan's power,
and rise when morning comes
to give you thanks and praise.

We ask this through our Lord Jesus Christ, your Son,
who lives and reigns with you and the Holy Spirit,
God, for ever and ever.

(Dismissal, p. 133)

FRIDAY MORNING

Reflection

ANYONE searching his own heart knows the deposits of darkness and sin lying there, despite God's gifts and grace. To recognize ourselves as sinners is simply to recognize that which is weakest in ourselves. No, we do not always act for the best motives, nor do we always think the best thoughts. Jealousy, resentment, selfishness surface too often for us to deny they are part of us.

Ultimately, only God can cleanse us of our sins. His mercy we seek in Psalm 51.

I must pray for my own sinfulness, but there is a sinfulness in the society where I live, in its institutions, its customs, its ways of acting, causing us to be alienated from our God. The Prophet Isaiah calls us to turn from our idols and our foolishness and seek our God who waits to reveal himself to us (cf. 45:15-25).

Every prayer for mercy is made with the certainty of being heard. "Make me hear rejoicing and gladness, that the bones you have crushed may revive." The final Psalm, Psalm 100, expresses our rejoicing and gladness. We can approach God confidently, through his Son, Jesus Christ. "We are his people, the sheep of his flock."

MORNING PRAYER

LORD, open my lips.
—And my mouth will proclaim your praise.
Glory to, etc.: —as it was, etc.

Antiphon

Come, let us give thanks to the Lord, for his great love is without end.

Invitatory psalm, p. 126.

Antiphon

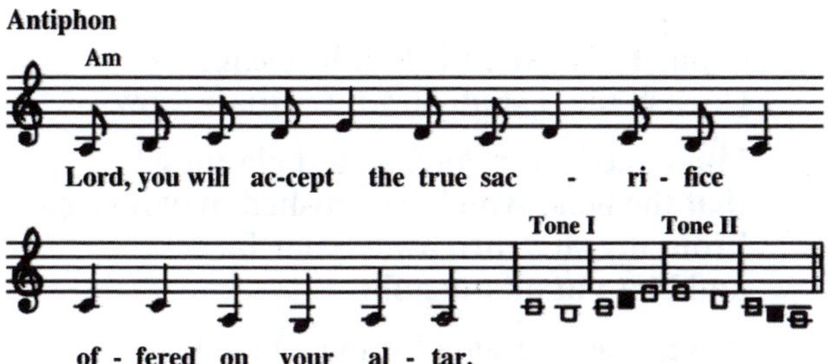

Psalm 51

O God, have mercy on me

Your inmost being must be renewed, and you must put on the new man (Ephesians 4:23-24).

HAVE mercy on me, God, in your kindness.
In your compassion blot out my offense.
O wash me more and more from my guilt
and cleanse me from my sin.

My offenses truly I know them;
my sin is always before me.

Against you, you alone, have I sinned;
what is evil in your sight I have done.

That you may be justified when you give sentence
and be without reproach when you judge.
O see, in guilt I was born,
a sinner was I conceived.

Indeed you love truth in the heart;
then in the secret of my heart teach me wisdom.
O purify me, then I shall be clean;
O wash me, I shall be whiter than snow.

Make me hear rejoicing and gladness,
that the bones you have crushed may revive.
From my sins turn away your face
and blot out all my guilt.

A pure heart create for me, O God,
put a steadfast spirit within me.
Do not cast me away from your presence,
nor deprive me of your holy spirit.

Give me again the joy of your help;
with a spirit of fervor sustain me,
that I may teach transgressors your ways
and sinners may return to you.

O rescue me, God, my helper,
and my tongue shall ring out your goodness.
O Lord, open my lips
and my mouth shall declare your praise.

For in sacrifice you take no delight,
burnt offering from me you would refuse,

my sacrifice, a contrite spirit.
A humbled, contrite heart you will not spurn.

In your goodness, show favor to Zion:
rebuild the walls of Jerusalem.
Then you will be pleased with lawful sacrifice,
holocausts offered on your altar.

Glory to the Father, and to the Son, and to the Holy Spirit:
as it was in the beginning, is now, and will be for ever. Amen.

Psalm-prayer

Father, he who knew no sin was made sin for us, to save us and restore us to your friendship. Look upon our contrite heart and afflicted spirit and heal our troubled conscience, so that in the joy and strength of the Holy Spirit we may proclaim your praise and glory before all the nations.

Antiphon

Psalm 100

The joyful song of those entering God's temple

The Lord calls his ransomed people to sing songs of victory (Saint Athanasius).

CRY out with joy to the Lord, all the earth.
Serve the Lord with gladness.
Come before him, singing for joy.

Know that he, the Lord, is God.
He made us, we belong to him,
we are his people, the sheep of his flock.

Go within his gates, giving thanks.
Enter his courts with songs of praise.
Give thanks to him and bless his name.

Indeed, how good is the Lord,
eternal his merciful love.
He is faithful from age to age.

Glory to the Father, and to the Son, and to the Holy Spirit:
as it was in the beginning, is now, and will be for ever. Amen.

Psalm-prayer

With joy and gladness we cry out to you, Lord, and ask you: open our hearts to sing your praises and announce your goodness and truth.

Reading

Ephesians 4:29-32

GUARD against foul talk; let your words be for the improvement of others, as occasion offers, and do good to your listeners, otherwise you will only be grieving the Holy Spirit of God who has marked you with his seal for you to be set free when the day comes. Never have grudges against others, or lose your temper, or raise your voice to anybody, or call each other names, or allow any sort of spitefulness. Be friends with one another, and kind, forgiving each other as readily as God forgave you in Christ.

Responsory

At daybreak, be merciful to me.
—At daybreak, be merciful to me.
Make known to me the path that I must walk.
—be merciful to me.
Glory to the Father, and to the Son, and to the Holy Spirit.
—At daybreak, be merciful to me.

Antiphon

The Lord has come to his people and set them free.

Canticle of Zechariah

The Messiah and his forerunner

BLESSED be the Lord, the God of Israel;
he has come to his people and set them free.

He has raised up for us a mighty savior,
born of the house of his servant David.

Through his holy prophets he promised of old
that he would save us from our enemies,
from the hands of all who hate us.

He promised to show mercy to our fathers
and to remember his holy covenant.

This was the oath he swore to our father Abraham:
to set us free from the hands of our enemies,
free to worship him without fear,
holy and righteous in his sight
all the days of our life.

You, my child, shall be called the prophet of the Most High;
for you will go before the Lord to prepare his way,
to give his people knowledge of salvation
by the forgiveness of their sins.

In the tender compassion of our God
the dawn from on high shall break upon us,
to shine on those who dwell in darkness and the shadow of death,
and to guide our feet into the way of peace.

Glory to the Father, and to the Son, and to the Holy Spirit:
as it was in the beginning, is now, and will be for ever. Amen.

(For music, turn to p. 131)

Intercessions

THROUGH his cross the Lord Jesus brought salvation to the human race. We adore him and in faith we call out to him:

Lord, pour out your mercy upon us.

Christ, Rising Sun, warm us with your rays,
—and restrain us from every evil impulse.
Keep guard over our thoughts, words and actions,
—and make us pleasing in your sight this day.
Turn your gaze from our sinfulness,
—and cleanse us from our iniquities.
Through your cross and resurrection,
—fill us with the consolation of the Spirit.

Our Father . . .

Prayer

GOD our Father,
you conquer the darkness of ignorance
by the light of your Word.
Strengthen within our hearts
the faith you have given us;
let not temptation ever quench the fire
that your love has kindled within us.

We ask this through our Lord Jesus Christ, your Son,
who lives and reigns with you and the Holy Spirit,
God, for ever and ever.

(Dismissal p. 133)

FRIDAY EVENING

Reflection

IN PSALM 41 the mind and heart of Jesus Christ during his passion are opened for us to see. With words from this Psalm Jesus spoke of his betrayal by Judas (Mark 14:18) *and his deliverance into the hands of enemies who hated him. At the same time, we see in this Psalm his confidence in the mercy and protection of his Father.*

The forgiveness and patience Jesus Christ offered to his betrayer and those who put him to death tell of God's mercy to us. Even though we are sinners, God has made an everlasting covenant of forgiveness with us.

The Lord of hosts is with us:
The God of Jacob is our stronghold.

This evening we celebrate God's mercy revealed in the passion of his Son, and we in turn are reminded to forgive those around us.

The reading from Romans, recalling the patient endurance of Jesus Christ, urges that "we who are strong [in faith] have a duty to put up with the qualms of the weak [in faith]."

EVENING PRAYER

GOD, come to my assistance.
—Lord, make haste to help me.
Glory to, etc.:—as it was, etc.

Antiphon

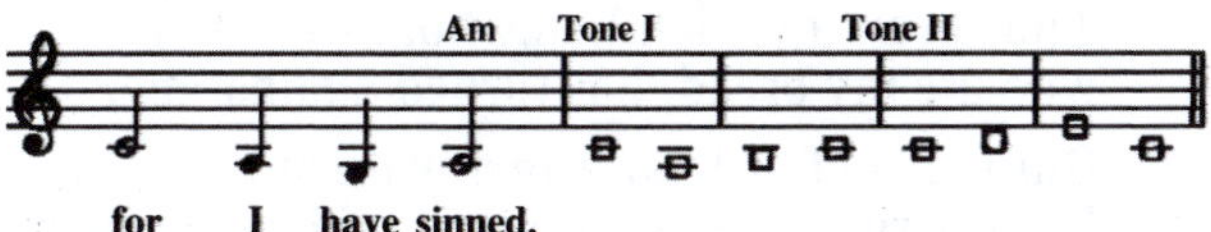

Psalm 41

Prayer of a sick person

One of you will betray me, yes, one who eats with me (Mark 14:18).

HAPPY the man who considers the poor and the weak.
The Lord will save him in the day of evil,
will guard him, give him life, make him happy in the land
and will not give him up to the will of his foes.
The Lord will help him on his bed of pain,
he will bring him back from sickness to health.

As for me, I said: "Lord, have mercy on me,
heal my soul for I have sinned against you."

My foes are speaking evil against me.
"How long before he dies and his name be forgotten?"
They come to visit me and speak empty words,
their hearts full of malice, they spread it abroad.

My enemies whisper together against me.
They all weigh up the evil which is on me:
"Some deadly thing has fastened upon him,
he will not rise again from where he lies."
Thus even my friend, in whom I trusted,
who ate my bread, has turned against me.

But you, O Lord, have mercy on me.
Let me rise once more and I will repay them.
By this I shall know that you are my friend,
if my foes do not shout in triumph over me.
If you uphold me I shall be unharmed
and set in your presence for evermore.

Blessed be the Lord, the God of Israel
from age to age. Amen. Amen.

Glory to the Father, and to the Son, and to the Holy Spirit:
as it was in the beginning, is now, and will be for ever. Amen.

Psalm-prayer

Lord Jesus, healer of soul and body, you said: Blessed are the merciful, they will obtain mercy. Teach us to come to the aid of the needy in a spirit of brotherly love, that we in turn may be received and strengthened by you.

Psalm 46

God our refuge and strength

He shall be called Emmanuel, which means: God with us (Matthew 1:23).

GOD is for us a refuge and strength,
a helper close at hand, in time of distress:
so we shall not fear though the earth should rock,
though the mountains fall into the depths of the sea,
even though its waters rage and foam,
even though the mountains be shaken by its waves.

The Lord of hosts is with us:
the God of Jacob is our stronghold.

The waters of a river give joy to God's city,
the holy place where the Most High dwells.
God is within, it cannot be shaken;
God will help it at the dawning of the day.
Nations are in tumult, kingdoms are shaken:
he lifts his voice, the earth shrinks away.

The Lord of hosts is with us:
the God of Jacob is our stronghold.

Come, consider the works of the Lord,
the redoubtable deeds he has done on the earth.
He puts an end to wars over all the earth;
the bow he breaks, the spear he snaps.
He burns the shields with fire.
"Be still and know that I am God,
supreme among the nations, supreme on the earth!"

The Lord of hosts is with us:
the God of Jacob is our stronghold.

Glory to the Father, and to the Son, and to the Holy Spirit:
as it was in the beginning, is now, and will be for ever. Amen.

Psalm-prayer

All-powerful Father, the refuge and strength of your people, you protect in adversity and defend in prosperity those who put their trust in you. May they persevere in seeking your will and find their way to you through obedience.

Reading

Romans 15: 1-3

WE WHO are strong have a duty to put up with the qualms of the weak without thinking of yourselves. Each of us should think of his neighbors and help them to become stronger

Christians. Christ did not think of himself: the words of scripture—*the insults of those who insult you fall on me*—apply to him.

Responsory

Christ loved us and washed away our sins, in his own blood.
—Christ loved us and washed away our sins, in his own blood.
He made us a nation of kings and priests,
—in his own blood.
Glory to the Father, and to the Son, and to the Holy Spirit.
—Christ loved us and washed away our sins, in his own blood.

Antiphon

The Lord has come to the help of his servants, for he has remembered his promise of mercy.

Canticle of Mary

The soul rejoices in the Lord

MY SOUL proclaims the greatness of the Lord,
my spirit rejoices in God my Savior
for he has looked with favor on his lowly servant.

From this day all generations will call me blessed:
the Almighty has done great things for me,
and holy is his Name.

He has mercy on those who fear him
in every generation.

He has shown the strength of his arm,
he has scattered the proud in their conceit.

He has cast down the mighty from their thrones,
and has lifted up the lowly.

He has filled the hungry with good things
and the rich he has sent away empty.

He has come to the help of his servant Israel
for he has remembered his promise of mercy,
the promise he made to our fathers,
to Abraham and his children for ever.

Glory to the Father, and to the Son, and to the Holy Spirit:
as it was in the beginning, is now, and will be for ever. Amen.

(For music, turn to p. 132)

Intercessions

BLESSED be God, who hears the prayers of the needy, and fills the hungry with good things. Let us pray to him in confidence:
Lord, show us your mercy.

Merciful Father, upon the cross Jesus offered you the perfect evening sacrifice,
—we pray now for all the suffering members of his Church.

Release those in bondage, give sight to the blind,
—shelter the widow and the orphan.

Clothe your faithful people in the armor of salvation,
—and shield them from the deceptions of the devil.

Let your merciful presence be with us, Lord, at the hour of our death,
—may we be found faithful and leave this world in your peace.
Lead the departed into the light of your dwelling-place,
—that they may gaze upon you for all eternity.

Our Father . . .

Prayer

GOD our Father,
help us to follow the example
of your Son's patience in suffering.
By sharing the burden he carries,
may we come to share his glory
in the kingdom where he lives with you and the Holy Spirit,
God, for ever and ever.

(Dismissal, p. 133)

SATURDAY MORNING

Reflection

AT THE center of this morning's prayer is the promise God made to his people through the Prophets: If they remained faithful to him and did his will, he would deliver them from their sins and their enemies. And the people often sang of the Lord's great mercy and power.

Delivered from the darkness of sin through Christ and re-created through the life-giving waters of baptism, Christians also praise God for his great deeds. God has redeemed us and guides us to his holy dwelling.

The promise of God, made long ago to his chosen people as he led them to salvation, is extended now to all nations. His love and faithfulness is offered to all (Psalm 117).

God's goodness, however, always waits for our response and acceptance.

MORNING PRAYER

LORD, open my lips.
—And my mouth will proclaim your praise.
Glory to, etc.: —as it was, etc.

Antiphon

Come, let us worship God who holds the world and its wonders in his creating hand.

Invitatory psalm, p. 126.

Antiphon

Psalm 119:145-152

XIX (Koph)

I CALL with all my heart; Lord, hear me,
I will keep your commands.
I call upon you, save me
and I will do your will.

I rise before dawn and cry for help,
I hope in your word.
My eyes watch through the night
to ponder your promise.

In your love hear my voice, O Lord:
give me life by your decrees.
Those who harm me unjustly draw near:
they are far from your law.

But you, O Lord, are close:
your commands are truth.

Long have I known that your will
is established for ever.

Glory to the Father, and to the Son, and to the Holy Spirit:
as it was in the beginning, is now, and will be for ever. Amen.

Psalm-prayer

Save us by the power of your hand, Father, for our enemies have ignored your words. May the fire of your word consume our sins and its brightness illumine our hearts.

Antiphon

Psalm 117

Praise for God's loving compassion

I affirm that . . . the Gentile peoples are to praise God because of his mercy (Romans 15:8-9).

O PRAISE the Lord, all you nations,
acclaim him, all you peoples!

Strong is his love for us;
he is faithful for ever.

Glory to the Father, and to the Son, and to the Holy Spirit:

as it was in the beginning, is now, and will be for ever. Amen.

Psalm-prayer

God our Father, may all nations and peoples praise you. May Jesus, who is called faithful and true and who lives with you eternally, possess our hearts for ever.

Reading

2 Peter 1:10-11

BROTHERS, you have been called and chosen: work all the harder to justify it. If you do all these things there is no danger that you will ever fall away. In this way you will be granted admittance into the eternal kingdom of our Lord and Savior Jesus Christ.

Responsory

I cry to you, O Lord, for you are my refuge.
—I cry to you, O Lord, for you are my refuge.
You are all I desire in the land of the living;
—for you are my refuge.
Glory to the Father, and to the Son, and to the Holy Spirit.
—I cry to you, O Lord, for you are my refuge.

Antiphon

Lord, shine on those who dwell in darkness and the shadow of death.

Canticle of Zechariah

The Messiah and his forerunner

BLESSED be the Lord, the God of Israel;
he has come to his people and set them free.

He has raised up for us a mighty savior,
born of the house of his servant David.

Through his holy prophets he promised of old
that he would save us from our enemies,
from the hands of all who hate us.

He promised to show mercy to our fathers
and to remember his holy covenant.

This was the oath he swore to our father Abraham:
to set us free from the hands of our enemies,
free to worship him without fear,
holy and righteous in his sight
all the days of our life.

You, my child, shall be called the prophet of the Most High;
for you will go before the Lord to prepare his way,
to give his people knowledge of salvation
by the forgiveness of their sins.

In the tender compassion of our God
the dawn from on high shall break upon us,
to shine on those who dwell in darkness and the shadow of death,
and to guide our feet into the way of peace.

Glory to the Father, and to the Son, and to the Holy Spirit:
as it was in the beginning, is now, and will be for ever. Amen.

(For music, turn to p. 131)

Intercessions

LET us all praise Christ. In order to become our faithful and merciful high priest before the Father's throne, he chose to become one of us, a brother in all things. In prayer we ask of him:
Lord, share with us the treasure of your love.

Sun of Justice, you filled us with light at our baptism,
—we dedicate this day to you.

At every hour of the day, we give you glory,
—in all our deeds, we offer you praise.

Mary, your mother, was obedient to your word,
—direct our lives in accordance with that word.

Our lives are surrounded with passing things; set our hearts on things of heaven,
—so that through faith, hope and charity we may come to enjoy the vision of your glory.

Our Father . . .

Prayer

LORD,
free us from the dark night of death.
Let the light of resurrection
dawn within our hearts
to bring us to the radiance of eternal life.

We ask this through our Lord Jesus Christ, your Son,
who lives and reigns with you and the Holy Spirit,
God, for ever and ever.

(Dismissal, p. 133)

COMMON PRAYERS

INVITATORY PSALM

Psalm 95

A call to praise God

Encourage each other while it is still today (Hebrews 3:13).

(The antiphon is recited and then repeated)

COME, let us sing to the Lord
and shout with joy to the Rock who saves us.
Let us approach him with praise and thanksgiving
and sing joyful songs to the Lord.

(Antiphon repeated)

The Lord is God, the mighty God,
the great king over all the gods.
He holds in his hands the depths of the earth
and the highest mountains as well.
He made the sea; it belongs to him,
the dry land, too, for it was formed by his hands.

(Antiphon repeated)

Come, then, let us bow down and worship,
bending the knee before the Lord, our maker.
For he is our God and we are his people,
the flock he shepherds.

(Antiphon repeated)

Today, listen to the voice of the Lord:
Do not grow stubborn, as your fathers did in the wilderness,
when at Meriba and Massah
they challenged me and provoked me,
although they had seen all of my works.

(Antiphon repeated)

Forty years I endured that generation.
I said, "They are a people whose hearts go astray
and they do not know my ways."
So I swore in my anger,
"They shall not enter into my rest."

(Antiphon repeated)

Glory to the Father, and to the Son, and to the Holy Spirit:
as it was in the beginning, is now, and will be for ever. Amen.

(Antiphon repeated)

In individual recitation, the antiphon may be said only at the beginning of the psalm; it need not be repeated after each strophe.

For alternative invitatory psalms, see p. 128.

The psalm with its antiphon may be omitted when the invitatory precedes Morning Prayer.

Alternative Invitatory Psalms

In place of psalm 95 one of the following three psalms may be said. And if the substituted psalm occurs in the Office, psalm 95 may be said in its place.

Psalm 100

The joyful song of those entering God's temple

The Lord calls his ransomed people to sing songs of victory (Saint Athanasius).

CRY out with joy to the Lord, all the earth.
Serve the Lord with gladness.
Come before him, singing for joy.

Know that he, the Lord, is God.
He made us, we belong to him,
we are his people, the sheep of his flock.

Go within his gates, giving thanks.
Enter his courts with songs of praise.
Give thanks to him and bless his name.

Indeed, how good is the Lord,
eternal his merciful love.
He is faithful from age to age.

Glory to the Father, and to the Son, and to the Holy Spirit:
as it was in the beginning, is now, and will be for ever. Amen.

Psalm 67

People of all nations will worship the Lord

You must know that God is offering his salvation to all the world (Acts 28:28).

O GOD, be gracious and bless us
and let your face shed its light upon us.
So will your ways be known upon earth
and all nations learn your saving help.

Let the peoples praise you, O God;
let all the peoples praise you.

Let the nations be glad and exult
for you rule the world with justice.

With fairness you rule the peoples,
you guide the nations on earth.

Let the peoples praise you, O God;
let all the peoples praise you.

The earth has yielded its fruit
for God, our God, has blessed us.
May God still give us his blessing
till the ends of the earth revere him.

Glory to the Father, and to the Son, and to the Holy Spirit:
as it was in the beginning, is now, and will be for ever. Amen.

Psalm 24

The Lord's entry into his temple

Christ opened heaven for us in the manhood he assumed (Saint Irenaeus).

THE Lord's is the earth and its fullness,
the world and all its peoples.
It is he who set it on the seas;
on the waters he made it firm.

Who shall climb the mountain of the Lord?
Who shall stand in his holy place?
The man with clean hands and pure heart,
who desires not worthless things,
who has not sworn so as to deceive his neighbor.

He shall receive blessings from the Lord
and reward from the God who saves him.
Such are the men who seek him,
seek the face of the God of Jacob.

O gates, lift high your heads;
grow higher, ancient doors.
Let him enter, the king of glory!

Who is the king of glory?
The Lord, the mighty, the valiant,
the Lord, the valiant in war.

O gates, lift high your heads;
grow higher, ancient doors.
Let him enter, the king of glory!

Who is he, the king of glory?
He, the Lord of armies,
he is the king of glory.

Glory to the Father, and to the Son, and to the Holy Spirit:
as it was in the beginning, is now, and will be for ever. Amen.

Canticle of Zechariah
The Messiah and his forerunner

1. Blessed be the Lord, the God —	of	Israel;
2. He has raised up for us a might -	y	savior,
3. Through his holy prophets he promised	of	old
4. He promised to show mercy to —	our	fathers
5. This was the oath he swore to our fa -	ther	Abraham:
6. Free to worship him with -	out	fear,
7. You, my child, shall be called the prophet of the	Most	High;
8. To give his people knowledge of —	sal -	vation
9. In the tender compassion of —	our	God
10. To shine on those who dwell in darkness and the shadow	of	death,
11. Glory to the Father, and to —	the	Son,
12. As it was in the —	be -	ginning,

1. he has come to his —	people and
2. born of the —	house of his
3. that he would save us from our —	enemies, from the hands of
4. and to re -	member his
5. to set us —	free from the hands
6. holy and righteous in his —	sight all the days
7. for you will go before the —	Lord to pre -
8. by the for -	giveness
9. the dawn from on —	high shall
10. and to guide our —	feet into the
11. and to —	the
12. is now, and —	will

1.	set	them	free.
2.	ser -	vant	David.
3.	all	who	hate us.
4.	ho -	ly	covenant.
5	of	our	enemies,
6.	of	our	life.
7.	pare	his	way,
8.	of	their	sins.
9.	break	up -	on us,
10.	way	of	peace.
11.	Hol -	ly	Spirit:
12.	be	for	ever. Amen.

Canticle of Mary

The soul rejoices in the Lord

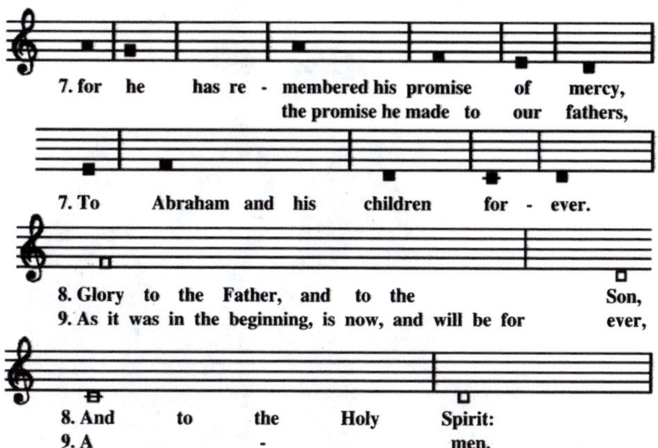

Dismissal

If a priest or deacon presides, he dismisses the people:

The Lord be with you.
—And also with you.
May almighty God bless you,
the Father, and the Son, and the Holy Spirit.
—Amen.

Another form of the blessing may be used, as at Mass.

Then he adds:

Go in peace.
—Thanks be to God.

In the absence of a priest or deacon and in individual recitation, the Prayer concludes:

May the Lord bless us,
protect us from all evil
and bring us to everlasting life.
—Amen.

"The spiritual life is not confined to participation in the liturgy. The Christian is assuredly called to pray with his brethren, but he must also enter into his chamber to pray to the Father in secret (cf. Matthew 6:6); indeed, according to the teaching of the Apostle Paul, he should pray without ceasing (cf. 1 Thessalonians 5:17)" (Vatican II: Constitution on the Sacred Liturgy, no. 12.)

HELPS FOR PRAYER

PRAYER is not just setting aside a set time for prayer every day. If prayer is no more than just a set time every day, we will never achieve a strong prayer life. Don't look at prayer in a vacuum, separated from the rest of life. A good prayer life needs a way of life throughout the day that allows us to find a stillness, a quiet time in the middle of our busy day. No matter how busy we are, we must pray.

To pray well, one of the first things we need to do is simply to slow down. Learn to pace our self better. Don't expect a good prayer life to happen at once. We don't just stumble upon it. We have to work at it and struggle with it. Prayer does not come easy to most of us.

It can be hard for us to think that we can just sit without saying anything, yet a friend is someone in whose presence we can stay quietly. Jesus Christ is our friend, and sometimes prayer is just sitting quietly, perfectly still in His presence. Don't think we have to always say something in prayer. Sometimes it is just sitting there in God's presence.

Prayer is also listening to God, in the words of Samuel, "Speak, Lord, your servant is listening." Don't think that when we pray we have to match the eloquence of St. Ambrose or Thomas Aquinas in the prayers which we include in this book. When we pray, don't be afraid of repeating our affections over and over again.

When we pray, forget everything else. Forget problems and plans for the week, different assignments and duties. Leave them all behind when we pray.

It is important to understand that we are not wasting our time when we pray. We are not being unproductive when we pray. Don't worry about some work that we have to do or phone call that we have to make. When we pray, leave all that behind. Nothing is more important than prayer. Prayer is the most important thing we can do for our spiritual life.

We make a big mistake if we pray only when we feel like praying. Daily prayer, and frequent daily prayer, purifies us, sets a prayerful tone to our day, and gets us in the habit of prayer so that when those difficult times do come, then we can pray easily.

There are times when we all feel that our prayers don't accomplish anything, and that life is at a standstill. We have prayed. We have asked. We have knocked. But nothing happened. The power of God in our lives is often like a slow, steady drip of the faucet or the hands of a clock. We don't see the movement, but it is there. We notice it only over the long run.

Finally, we learn to pray by praying. We must give it time when we are most alert and full of energy, not just the left over periods at the end of the day. If we drag our self to prayer after a long day,

and we drift off while we pray, don't blame it on prayer. Spend fifteen minutes a day of prime time in prayer and being alone with the Lord, and we will learn more about prayer than anyone could ever teach us.

Father John Murray, C.Ss.R.

"Christ conquers! Christ reigns! Christ commands!"

READINGS, PRAYERS, and DEVOTIONS on the Mysteries of Christ

ADVENT

Poem: The Incarnation

THEN He summoned an archangel,
Saint Gabriel: and when he came,
Sent him forth to find a maiden,
    Mary was her name.

Only through her consenting love
Could the mystery be preferred
That the Trinity in human
    Flesh might clothe the Word.

Though the three Persons worked the wonder
It only happened in the One.
So was the Word made incarnation
    In Mary's womb, a son.

So He who only had a Father
Now had a Mother undefiled,
Though not as ordinary maids
    Had she conceived the Child.

By Mary, and with her own flesh
He was clothed in His own frame:
Both Son of God and Son of Man
    Together had one name.

Saint John of the Cross: Translator: Roy Campbell

Announcement of the Birth of Jesus

Luke 1:26-38

IN THE sixth month, the angel Gabriel was sent by God to a town in Galilee called Nazareth, to a virgin betrothed to a man named Joseph, of the house of David. The virgin's name was Mary.

The angel came to her and said, "Hail, full of grace! The Lord is with you." But she was greatly troubled by his words and wondered in her heart what this salutation could mean.

Then the angel said to her, "Do not be afraid, Mary, for you have found favor with God. Behold, you will conceive in your womb and bear a son, and you will name him Jesus. He will be great and will be called Son of the Most High. The Lord God will give him the throne of his ancestor David. He will rule over the house of Jacob forever, and of his kingdom there will be no end."

Mary said to the angel, "How will this be, since I am a virgin?" The angel answered, "The Holy Spirit will come upon you, and the power of the Most High will overshadow you. Therefore, the child to be born will be holy, and he will be called the Son of God. And behold, your cousin Elizabeth in her old age has also conceived a son, and she who was called barren is now in her sixth month, for nothing will be impossible for God."

Then Mary said, "Behold, I am the servant of the Lord. Let it be done to me according to your word." After this, the angel departed from her.

God's Word will come to us

Bernard: *Sermons*

WE KNOW that there are three comings of the Lord. The third lies between the other two. It is invisible, while the other two are visible. In the first coming he was seen on earth, dwelling among men; he himself testifies that they saw him and hated him. In the final coming *all flesh will see the salvation of our God* and *they will look on him whom they pierced.* The intermediate coming is a hidden one; in it only the elect see the Lord within their own selves, and they are saved. In his first coming our Lord came in our flesh and in our weakness; in this middle coming he comes in spirit and in power; in the final coming he will be seen in glory and majesty.

Because this coming lies between the other two, it is like a road on which we travel from the first coming to the last. In the first, Christ was our redemption, in the last, he will appear as our life; in this middle coming, he is our rest and consolation.

In case someone should think that what we say about this middle coming is sheer invention, listen to what our Lord himself says: *If anyone loves me, he will keep my word, and my Father will love him, and we will come to him.* There is another passage of Scripture which reads: *He who fears God will do good,* but something further has been said about the one who loves, that is, that he will keep God's word. Where is God's word to be kept? Obviously in the heart, as the prophet says: *I have hidden your words in my heart, so that I may not sin against you.*

Keep God's word in this way. Let it enter into your very being, let it take possession of your desires and your whole way of life. Feed on goodness, and your soul will delight in its richness. Remember to eat your bread, or your heart will wither away. Fill your soul with richness and strength.

Prayer

GRANT your faithful, we pray, almighty God, the resolve to run forth to meet your Christ
with righteous deeds at his coming,
so that, gathered at his right hand,
they may be worthy to possess the heavenly Kingdom.
Through our Lord Jesus Christ, your Son,
who lives and reigns with you in the unity of the Holy Spirit,
God, for ever and ever.

(Collect, 1st Sun. of Advent)

CHRISTMAS TIME

Birth of Jesus

Luke 2:1-14

IN THOSE days, a decree was issued by Caesar Augustus that a census should be taken throughout the entire world. This was the first such registration, and it took place when Quirinius was governor of Syria.

Everyone traveled to his own town to be enrolled. Joseph therefore went from the town of Nazareth in Galilee to Judea, to the city of David called Bethlehem, because he was of the house and family of David. He went to be registered together with Mary, his betrothed, who was expecting a child. While they were there, the time came for her to have her child, and she gave birth to her firstborn son. She wrapped him in swaddling clothes and laid him in a manger, because there was no room for them in the inn.

In the nearby countryside there were shepherds living in the fields and keeping watch over their flock throughout the night. Suddenly, an angel of the Lord appeared to them, and the glory of the Lord shone around them. They were terror-stricken, but the angel said to them, "Do not be afraid, for I bring you good news of great joy for all the people. For this day in the city of David there has been born to you a Savior who is Christ, the Lord.

This will be a sign for you: you will find an infant wrapped in swaddling clothes and lying in a manger." And suddenly there was with the angel a multitude of the heavenly host, praising God and saying,

"Glory to God in the highest heaven,
and on earth peace to all those on whom his favor rests."

Christian, remember your dignity

Leo the Great: *Sermon*

DEARLY beloved, today our Savior is born; let us rejoice. Sadness should have no place on the birthday of life. The fear of death has been swallowed up; life brings us joy with the promise of eternal happiness.

No one is shut out from this joy; all share the same reason for rejoicing. Our Lord, victor over sin and death, finding no man free from sin, came to free us all. Let the saint rejoice as he sees the palm of victory at hand. Let the sinner be glad as he receives the offer of forgiveness. Let the pagan take courage as he is summoned to life.

In the fullness of time, chosen in the unfathomable depths of God's wisdom, the Son of God took for himself our common humanity in order to reconcile it with its creator. He came to overthrow the devil, the origin of death, in that very nature by which he had overthrown mankind.

And so at the birth of our Lord the angels sing in joy: *Glory to God in the highest*, and they proclaim *peace to his people on earth* as they see the heavenly Jerusalem being built from all the nations of the world. When the angels on high are so exultant at this marvelous work of God's goodness, what joy should it not bring to the lowly hearts of men?

Beloved, let us give thanks to God the Father, through his Son, in the Holy Spirit, because in his great love for us he took pity on us, *and when we were dead in our sins he brought us to life with Christ,* so that in him we might be a new creation. Let us throw off our old nature and all its ways and, as we have come to birth in Christ, let us renounce the works of the flesh.

Christian, remember your dignity, and now that you share in God's own nature, do not return by sin to your former base condition. Bear in mind who is your head and of whose body you are a member. Do not forget that you have been rescued from the power of darkness and brought into the light of God's kingdom.

Through the sacrament of baptism you have become a temple of the Holy Spirit. Do not drive away so great a guest by evil conduct and become again a slave to the devil, for your liberty was bought by the blood of Christ.

Prayer

GRANT, we pray, almighty God,
that, as we are bathed in the new radiance of your incarnate Word,
the light of faith, which illumines our minds,
may also shine through in our deeds.
Through our Lord Jesus Christ, your Son,
who lives and reigns with you in the unity of the Holy Spirit,
God, for ever and ever.

(Collect, The Nativity of the Lord [Christmas], Mass at Dawn)

Circumcision of Jesus

Luke 2:16-21

[THE shepherds] set off in haste [to Bethlehem] and found Mary and Joseph, and the baby lying in a manger.

When they saw the child, they recounted the message that had been told them about him. All who heard it were amazed at what the shepherds said to them. As for Mary, she treasured all these words and pondered them in her heart. And the shepherds went back, glorifying and praising God for all they had heard and seen, just as they had been told.

On the eighth day, when the time for the child's circumcision had arrived, he was given the name Jesus, the name the angel had given him before he had been conceived in the womb.

Prayer

O GOD, who through the fruitful virginity of Blessed Mary
bestowed on the human race
the grace of eternal salvation,
grant, we pray,
that we may experience the intercession of her,
through whom we were found worthy
to receive the author of life,
our Lord Jesus Christ, your Son.
Who lives and reigns with you in the unity of the Holy Spirit,
God, for ever and ever.

(Collect, Solemnity of Mary, the Holy Mother of God)

The Magi

Matthew 2:1-12

AFTER Jesus had been born in Bethlehem of Judea during the reign of King Herod, wise men traveled from the east and arrived in Jerusalem, inquiring, "Where is the newborn king of the Jews? We saw the rising of his star, and we have come to pay him homage."

On hearing about their inquiry, King Herod was greatly troubled, as was true of the whole of Jerusalem. Therefore, he summoned all the chief priests and the scribes and questioned them about where the Christ was to be born. They replied, "In Bethlehem of Judea, for thus has the prophet written:

'And you, Bethlehem, in the land of Judah,
are by no means least among the rulers of Judah,
for from you shall come a ruler
who will shepherd my people Israel.'"

Then Herod secretly summoned the wise men, and he ascertained from them the exact time of the star's appearance, after which he sent them on to Bethlehem, saying: "Go forth and search diligently for the child. When you have found him, bring me word, so that I can go and pay him homage."

After receiving these instructions from the king, the wise men set out. And behold, the star that they had seen at its rising proceeded ahead of them until it stopped over the place where the child was. The sight of the star filled them with great joy, and when they entered the house they beheld the child with Mary his mother. Falling to their knees, they paid him homage. Then they opened their treasure chests and offered him gifts of gold, frankincense, and myrrh. And since they had been warned in a dream not to return to Herod, they departed for their own country by another route.

In choosing to be born for us, God chose to be known by us

Peter Chrysologus: *Sermon*

IN THE mystery of our Lord's incarnation there were clear indications of his eternal Godhead. Yet the great events we celebrate today disclose and reveal in different ways the fact that God himself took a human body. Mortal man, enshrouded always in darkness, must not be left in ignorance, and so be deprived of what he can understand and retain only by grace.

In choosing to be born for us, God chose to be known by us. He therefore reveals himself in this way, in order that this great sacrament of his love may not be an occasion for us of great misunderstanding.

Today the Magi find, crying in a manger, the one they have followed as he shone in the sky. Today the Magi see clearly, in swaddling clothes, the one they have long awaited as he lay hidden among the stars.

Today the Magi gaze in deep wonder at what they see: heaven on earth, earth in heaven, man in God, God in man, one whom the whole universe cannot contain now enclosed in a tiny body. As they look, they believe and do not question, as their symbolic gifts bear witness: incense for God, gold for a king, myrrh for one who is to die.

So the Gentiles, who were the last, become the first: the faith of the Magi is the first fruits of the belief of the Gentiles.

Prayer

O GOD, who on this day
revealed your Only Begotten Son to the nations
by the guidance of a star,
grant in your mercy
that we, who know you already by faith,
may be brought to behold the beauty of your sublime glory.
Through our Lord Jesus Christ, your Son,
who lives and reigns with you in the unity of the Holy Spirit,
God, for ever and ever.

(Collect, Solemnity of the Epiphany of the Lord, Mass during the Day)

The finding in the temple

Luke 2:41-52

EVERY year his parents used to go to Jerusalem for the feast of Passover. And when Jesus was twelve years old, they made the journey as usual for the feast. When the days of the feast were over and they set off for home, the boy Jesus stayed behind in Jerusalem. His parents were not aware of this. Assuming that he was somewhere in the group of travelers, they journeyed for a day. Then they started to look for him among their relatives and friends, but when they failed to find him, they returned to Jerusalem to search for him.

After three days they found him in the temple, where he was sitting among the teachers, listening to them and asking them questions. And all who heard him were amazed at his intelligence and his answers. When they saw him, they were astonished, and his mother said to him: "Son, why have you done this to us? Your father and I have been searching for you with great anxiety." Jesus said to them, "Why were you searching for me? Did you not know that I must be in my Father's house?" But they did not comprehend what he said to them.

Then he went down with them and came to Nazareth, and he was obedient to them. His mother pondered all these things in her heart. And Jesus increased in wisdom and in age and in grace with God and men.

Prayer

O GOD, who were pleased to give us
the shining example of the Holy Family,
graciously grant that we may imitate them
in practicing the virtues of family life and in the bonds of charity,
and so, in the joy of your house,
delight one day in eternal rewards.
Through our Lord Jesus Christ, your Son,
who lives and reigns with you in the unity of the Holy Spirit,
God, for ever and ever.

(Collect, Feast of the Holy Family of Jesus, Mary and Joseph)

LENT

Mark 1:12-15

THE Spirit immediately drove him out into the desert. He remained there for forty days, during which time he was tempted by Satan. He lived there among the wild beasts, while the angels ministered to him.

After John had been arrested, Jesus came to Galilee proclaiming the gospel of God, and saying, "The time of fulfillment has arrived, and the kingdom of God is close at hand. Repent, and believe in the gospel."

In Christ we suffered temptation, and in him we overcame the devil

Augustine: *Commentary on the Psalms*

OUR pilgrimage on earth cannot be exempt from trial. We progress by means of trial. No one knows himself except through trial, or receives a crown except after victory, or strives except against an enemy or temptations.

The one who cries from the ends of the earth is in anguish, but is not left on his own. Christ chose to foreshadow us, who are his body, by means of his body, in which he has died, risen and ascended into heaven, so that the members of his body may hope to follow where their head has gone before.

He made us one with him when he chose to be tempted by Satan. We have heard in the gospel how the Lord Jesus Christ was tempted by the devil in the wilderness. Certainly Christ was tempted by the devil. In Christ you were tempted, for Christ received his flesh from your nature, but by his own power gained salvation for you; he suffered death in your nature, but by his own power gained life for you; he suffered insults in your nature, but by his own power gained glory for you, therefore, he suffered temptation in your nature, but by his own power gained victory for you.

If in Christ we have been tempted, in him we overcome the devil. Do you think only of Christ's temptations and fail to think of his victory? See yourself as tempted in him, and see yourself as victorious in him.

Prayer

GRANT, almighty God,
through the yearly observances of holy Lent,
that we may grow in understanding
of the riches hidden in Christ
and by worthy conduct pursue their effects.
Through our Lord Jesus Christ, your Son,
who lives and reigns with you in the unity of the Holy Spirit,
God, for ever and ever.

(Collect, 1st Sun. of Lent)

"Lord, by your cross and resurrection, you have set us free. You are the Savior of the world."

STATIONS OF THE CROSS (St. Alphonsus)

IN THE name of the Father, and the Son, and the Holy Spirit. Amen.

My Lord Jesus Christ, * you have made this journey to die for me with love unutterable, * and I have so many times unworthily abandoned you; * But now I love you with my whole heart, * and because I love you, * I repent sincerely for having ever offended you. * Pardon me, my God, * and let me go with you on this journey, * You go to die for love of me; * I wish also, my beloved Redeemer, to die for love of you. * My Jesus, I will live and die always united to you.

FIRST STATION

Jesus is condemned to death

Leader: We adore you, O Christ, and we bless you.

ALL: By your Holy Cross you have redeemed the world.

Leader: See how Jesus, after having been scourged and crowned with thorns, was unjustly condemned by Pilate to die on the Cross.

ALL: My adorable Jesus, it was not Pilate, * no, it was my sins, that condemned you to die. * By the merits of this sorrowful journey, * assist my soul in its journey toward eternity.* I love you, my blessed Jesus, * I love you more than myself; * I repent with my whole heart of having offended you. * Never let me separate myself from you again. * May I love you always; and then do with me what you will.

SECOND STATION

Jesus is made to bear his Cross

Leader: We adore you O Christ, and we bless you.

ALL: By your Holy Cross you have redeemed the world.

Leader: See how Jesus, in making this journey with the Cross on his shoulders, thought of us, and offered for us to his Father the death he was about to undergo.

ALL: My most beloved Jesus! * I embrace all the trials you have destined for me until death. * By the merits of the pain you suffered in carrying your Cross, * give me the necessary help to carry mine with perfect patience and resignation. * I love you, Jesus my Love, above all things; * I repent with my whole heart of having offended you. * Never let me separate myself from you again. * May I love you always * and then do with me as you will.

THIRD STATION

Jesus falls the first time

Leader: We adore you, O Christ, and we bless you.

ALL: By your Holy Cross you have redeemed the world.

Leader: See this first fall of Jesus under his Cross. His flesh was torn by the scourges, his head crowned with thorns, and he had lost a great quantity of blood. He was so weakened he could scarcely walk, and yet he had to carry this great load upon his shoulders. The soldiers struck him cruelly and he fell several times in his journey.

ALL: My beloved Jesus, * it is not the weight of the Cross, but of my sins, * that has made you suffer so much pain. * By this first fall, * keep me from the tragedy of falling into mortal sin.* I love you, O my Jesus, with my whole heart; * I repent of having offended you.* Never let me offend you again. * May I love you always; then do with me as you will.

FOURTH STATION

Jesus meets his afflicted Mother

Leader: We adore you, O Christ, and we bless you.

ALL: By your Holy Cross you have redeemed the world.

Leader: See the meeting of the Son and the Mother, which took place on this journey. Jesus and Mary looked at each other, and their looks became as so many arrows to wound those hearts which loved each other so tenderly.

ALL: My most loving Jesus, * by the sorrow you felt in this meeting,* grant me the grace of a great love for your most holy Mother. * And you, my Queen, overwhelmed with sorrow, * obtain for me by your intercession * a constant and tender remembrance of the Passion of your Son. *I love you, Jesus my Love; * I am sorry for ever having offended you. * Never let me offend you again. * May I love you always; and then do with me what you will.

FIFTH STATION

Simon helps Jesus to carry the Cross

Leader: We adore you, O Christ, and we bless you.

ALL: By your Holy Cross you have redeemed the world.

Leader: See how the Jews, seeing that at each stop Jesus was on the point of expiring, and fearing he would die on the way, when they wished him to die the shameful death of the Cross, forced Simon the Cyrenean to carry the Cross behind our Lord.

ALL: My most beloved Jesus, * I will not refuse the Cross as the Cyrenean did, * I accept it, I embrace it. * I accept in particular the death you have destined for me, * with all the pains which may come with it. * I unite it to your death, I offer it to you. * You have died for love of me; * I will die for love of you and to please you. * Help me by your grace. * I love you, Jesus, my Love, above all things; * Never let me separate myself from you again. * May I love you and I repent of ever having offended you. * Never let me offend you again. * May I love you always; and then do with me what you will.

SIXTH STATION

Veronica wipes the face of Jesus

Leader: We adore you, O Christ, and we bless you.

ALL: By your Holy Cross you have redeemed the world.

Leader: See how the holy woman named Veronica, seeing Jesus so afflicted, and his face bathed in sweat and blood, gave him a towel, with which he wiped his adorable face, leaving on it the impression of his holy countenance.

ALL: My most beloved Jesus, * your face was beautiful before,* but in this journey it has lost all its beauty,* and wounds and blood have disfigured it. * My soul also was once beautiful,* when it received your grace in Baptism,* but I have disfigured it since by my sins.* You alone, my Redeemer, can restore it to its former beauty.* Do this by your Passion, and then do with me what you will.

SEVENTH STATION

Jesus falls the second time

Leader: We adore you, O Christ, and we bless you.

ALL: By your Holy Cross you have redeemed the world.

Leader: Consider the second fall of Jesus under the Cross, a fall which renews the pain of all the wounds of the head and members of our afflicted Lord.

ALL: My most gentle Jesus, * how many times have you pardoned me,* and how many times have I fallen again, and begun again to offend you! By this new fall, * give me the necessary help to persevere in your grace until death. * In all temptations which assail me, * may I always commend myself to you. * I love you, Jesus my Love, with my whole heart. * I repent of having offended you. * May I love you always; and then do with me what you will.

EIGHTH STATION

Jesus meets the women of Jerusalem

Leader: We adore you, O Christ, and we bless you.

ALL: By your Holy Cross you have redeemed the world.

Leader: See how those women wept with compassion at seeing Jesus in such a state. He streamed with blood as he walked along. But Jesus said to them, "Weep not for me, but for your children."

ALL: My Jesus, laden with sorrows, * I weep for the offenses I have committed against you, * because of the pains they have deserved, * and still more because of the displeasure they have caused you, * who have loved me so much. * It is your love, * more than the fear of hell, * that causes me to weep for my sins. * My Jesus, I love you more than myself; * I repent of having offended you. *

Never let me offend you again. * May I love you always; then do with me what you will.

NINTH STATION

Jesus falls the third time

Leader: We adore you, O Christ, and we bless you.

ALL: By your Holy Cross you have redeemed the world.

Leader: See the third fall of Jesus Christ. His weakness was extreme, and the cruelty of his executioners excessive, who tried to hasten his steps when he had scarcely strength to move.

ALL: My outraged Jesus, * by the weakness you suffered in going to Calvary, * give me strength sufficient to conquer all human respect, * and all my wicked passions, which have led me to despise your friendship. * I love you, Jesus my Love, with my whole heart; * I am sorry for having offended you. * Never let me offend you again. * Grant that I may love you always; then do with me what you will.

TENTH STATION

Jesus is stripped of his garments

Leader: We adore you, O Christ, and we bless you.

ALL: By your Holy Cross you have redeemed the world.

Leader: See the violence with which the executioners stripped Jesus. His inner garments stuck to his torn flesh, and they dragged them off so roughly that the skin came with them. Pity your Savior so cruelly treated, and say to him:

ALL: My innocent Jesus, * by the torment you have felt, * help me to strip myself of all affection to things of earth, * that I may place all my love in you, * who are so worthy of my love. * I love you, O Jesus, with my whole heart; * I repent of having offended you. * Never let me offend you again. * May I love you always; and then do with me as you will.

ELEVENTH STATION

Jesus is nailed to the Cross

Leader: We adore you, O Christ, and we bless you.

ALL: By your Holy Cross you have redeemed the world.

Leader: See how Jesus was thrown on the Cross. He stretched out his hands and offered to his Eternal Father the sacrifice of his life for our salvation. These barbarians fastened him with nails, raised the Cross and left him to die with anguish and pain.

ALL: My Jesus, loaded with contempt, * nail my heart to your feet, * that it may stay there, * to love you and never leave you again. * I love you more than myself; I am sorry for having offended you again. * May I love you always; and then do with me what you will.

TWELFTH STATION

Jesus dies on the Cross

Leader: We adore you, O Christ, and we bless you.

ALL: By your Holy Cross you have redeemed the world.

Leader: See how your Jesus, after three hours' agony on the Cross, consumed in pain, abandons himself to the weight of his body, bows his head and dies.

ALL: (Moment of Silence) O my dying Jesus, * I kiss devoutly the Cross on which you died for love of me. * I deserve by my sins to die a miserable death, * but your death is my hope. * By your death, * give me grace to die embracing your feet, * and burning with love for you. * I yield my soul into your hands. * I love you with my whole heart. * I repent of ever having offended you. * Never let me offend you again. * May I love you always and then do with me what you will.

THIRTEENTH STATION

Jesus is taken from the Cross

Leader: We adore you, O Christ, and we bless you.

ALL: By your Holy Cross you have redeemed the world.

Leader: After our Lord died, two of his disciples, Joseph and Nicodemus, took him down from the Cross and placed him in the arms of his afflicted Mother, who received him with unutterable tenderness and pressed him to her bosom.

ALL: O Mother of Sorrows, * for the love of this Son, * accept me for your servant and pray to him for me. * And you, my Redeemer, since you have died for me, * let me love you; for I want you and nothing more. * I love you, my Jesus, * and I am sorry for ever having offended you. * Grant that I may love you always; and then do with me what you will.

FOURTEENTH STATION

Jesus is placed in the tomb

Leader: We adore you, O Christ, and we bless you.

ALL: By your Holy Cross you have redeemed the world.

Leader: See how the disciples carried the body of Jesus to bury it, accompanied by his holy Mother, who arranged it in the sepulcher with her own hands. Then they closed the tomb and all withdrew.

ALL: My buried Jesus, * I kiss the stone that encloses you. * But you did rise again on the third day. * By your resurrection, * make me rise glorious with you at the last day, * to be always united

with you in heaven, * to praise you and love you for ever. * I love you, and I repent of ever having offended you. * Never let me offend you again. * May I love you always; and then do with me what you will.

HOLY WEEK

Jesus' entry into Jerusalem

John 12:12-16

THE next day the great crowd of people who had come for the feast heard that Jesus was on his way to Jerusalem. Thus, they went out to meet him, carrying branches of palm and shouting,

"Hosanna!
Blessed is he who comes in the name of the Lord,
the King of Israel."

Jesus found a young donkey and rode it, as it is written,

"Do not be afraid, daughter of Zion.
Behold, your King is coming,
riding on a donkey's colt."

At first, his disciples did not understand this, but later, when Jesus had been glorified, they recalled that these things had been written about him and had happened to him.

Blessed is he who comes in the name of the Lord. Blessed is he the king of Israel.

Andrew of Crete: *Sermon*

LET us go together to meet Christ on the Mount of Olives. Today he returns from Bethany and proceeds of his own free will toward his holy and blessed passion, to consummate the mystery of our salvation. He who came down from heaven to raise us from the depths of sin, to raise us with himself, we are told in Scripture, *above every sovereignty, authority and power, and every other name that can be named,* now comes of his own free will to make his journey to Jerusalem. He comes without pomp or ostentation. As the psalmist says: *He will not dispute or raise his voice to make it heard in the streets.* He will be meek and humble, and he will make his entry in simplicity.

Let us run to accompany him as he hastens toward his passion, and imitate those who met him then, not by covering his path with garments, olive branches or palms, but by doing all we can to prostrate ourselves before him by being humble and by trying to live as he would wish. Then we shall be able to receive the Word at his coming, and God, whom no limits can contain, will be within us.

In his humility Christ entered the dark regions of our fallen world and he is glad that he became so humble for our sake, glad that he came and lived among us and shared in our nature in order to raise us up again to himself. And even though we are told that he has now ascended above the highest heavens—the proof, surely, of his power and godhead—his love for man will never rest until he has raised our earthbound nature from glory to glory, and made it one with his own in heaven.

So let us spread before his feet, not garments or soulless olive branches, which delight the eye for a few hours and then wither, but ourselves, clothed in his grace, or rather, clothed completely in him. We who have been baptized into Christ must ourselves be the garments that we spread before him. Now that the crimson stains of our sins have been washed away in the saving waters of baptism and we have become white as pure wool, let us present the conqueror of death, not with mere branches of palms but with the real rewards of his victory. Let our souls take the place of welcoming branches as we join today in the children's holy song: *Blessed is he who comes in the name of the Lord. Blessed is the king of Israel.*

Prayer

ALMIGHTY ever-living God,
who as an example of humility for the human race to follow
caused our Savior to take flesh and submit to the Cross,
graciously grant that we may heed his lesson of patient suffering
and so merit a share in his Resurrection.
Who lives and reigns with you in the unity of the Holy Spirit,
God, for ever and ever.

(Collect, Palm Sunday of the Passion of the Lord)

The lamb that was slain has delivered us from death and given us life

Melito of Sardis: *Easter homily*

THERE was much proclaimed by the prophets about the mystery of the Passover: that mystery is Christ, and to him be glory for ever and ever. Amen.

For the sake of suffering humanity he came down from heaven to earth, clothed himself in that humanity in the Virgin's womb, and was born a man. Having then a body capable of suffering, he took the pain of fallen man upon himself; he triumphed over the diseases of soul and body that were its cause, and by his Spirit, which was incapable of dying, he dealt man's destroyer, death, a fatal blow.

He was led forth like a lamb; he was slaughtered like a sheep. He ransomed us from our servitude to the world, as he had ransomed Israel from the land of Egypt; he freed us from our slavery to the devil, as he had freed Israel from the hand of Pharaoh. He sealed our souls with his own Spirit, and the members of our body with his own blood.

He is the One who covered death with shame and cast the devil into mourning, as Moses cast Pharaoh into mourning. He is the One who smote sin and robbed iniquity of offspring, as Moses robbed the Egyptians of their offspring. He is the One who brought us out of slavery into freedom, out of darkness into light, out of death into life, out of tyranny into an eternal kingdom; who made us a new priesthood, a people chosen to be his own for ever. He is the Passover that is our salvation.

It is he who endured every kind of suffering in all those who foreshadowed him. In Abel he was slain, in Isaac bound, in Jacob exiled, in Joseph sold, in Moses exposed to die. He was sacrificed in the Passover lamb, persecuted in David, dishonored in the prophets.

It is he who was made man of the Virgin, he who was hung on the tree; it is he who was buried in the earth, raised from the dead, and taken up to the heights of heaven. He is the mute lamb, the slain lamb, the lamb born of Mary, the fair ewe. He was seized from the flock, dragged off to be slaughtered, sacrificed in the evening, and buried at night. On the tree no bone of his was broken; in the earth his body knew no decay. He is the One who rose from the dead, and who raised man from the depths of the tomb.

Prayer

REMEMBER your mercies, O Lord,
and with your eternal protection sanctify
your servants,
for whom Christ your Son,
by the shedding of his Blood,
established the Paschal Mystery.
Who lives and reigns for ever and ever.

(Prayer, Friday of the Passion of the Lord [Good Friday])

EASTER TIME

The women at the tomb

Luke 24:1-12

AT DAYBREAK on the first day of the week, the women came to the tomb with the spices they had prepared. They found the stone rolled away from the tomb, but when they went inside, they did not find the body of the Lord Jesus.

While they stood there wondering about this, suddenly two men in dazzling clothes appeared at their side. They were terrified and bowed their faces to the ground, but the men said to them, "Why do you look among the dead for one who is alive? He is not here. He has been raised. Remember what he told you while he was still in Galilee: that the Son of Man must be handed over to sinners and be crucified and rise again on the third day." Then they recalled his words.

When they returned from the tomb, they reported all these things to the Eleven and to all the others. It was Mary Magdalene, Joanna, Mary the mother of James, and the other women with them who told this to the apostles. However, this story

of theirs seemed to be nonsense, and the apostles did not believe them. Nonetheless, Peter got up and ran to the tomb. Bending over, he looked inside and saw only the linen cloths. Then he returned home, wondering what had occurred.

The cross of Christ gives life to the human race

Ephrem: *Sermon*

DEATH trampled our Lord underfoot, but he in his turn treated death as a highroad for his own feet. He submitted to it, enduring it willingly, because by this means he would be able to destroy death in spite of itself. Death had its own way when our Lord went out from Jerusalem carrying his cross; but when by a loud cry from that cross he summoned the dead from the underworld, death was powerless to prevent it.

Death slew him by means of the body which he had assumed, but that same body proved to be the weapon with which he conquered death. Concealed beneath the cloak of his manhood, his godhead engaged death in combat; but in slaying our Lord, death itself was slain. It was able to kill natural human life, but was itself killed by the life that is above the nature of man.

Death could not devour our Lord unless he possessed a body, neither could hell swallow him up unless he bore our flesh; and so he came in search of a chariot in which to ride to the underworld. This chariot was the body which he received from the Virgin; in it he invaded death's fortress, broke open its strongroom and scattered all its treasure.

At length he came upon Eve, the mother of all the living. She was that vineyard whose enclosure her own hands had enabled death to violate, so that she could taste its fruit; thus the mother of all the living became the source of death for every living creature. But in her stead Mary grew up, a new vine in place of the old. Christ, the new life, dwelt within her. When death, with its customary imprudence, came foraging for her mortal fruit, it encountered its own destruction in the hidden life that fruit contained. All unsuspecting, it swallowed him up, and in so doing released life itself and set free a multitude of men.

He who was also the carpenter's glorious son set up his cross above death's all-consuming jaws, and led the human race into the dwelling place of life. Since a tree had brought about the downfall of mankind, it was upon a tree that mankind crossed over to the realm of life. Bitter was the branch that had once been grafted upon that ancient tree, but sweet the young shoot that has now been grafted in, the shoot in which we are meant to recognize the Lord whom no creature can resist.

We give glory to you, Lord, who raised up your cross to span the jaws of death like a bridge by which souls might pass from the region of the dead to the land of the living. We give glory to you who put on the body of a single mortal man and made it the source of life for every other mortal man. You are incontestably alive. Your murderers sowed your living body in the earth as farmers sow grain, but it sprang up and yielded an abundant harvest of men raised from the dead.

Come then, my brothers and sisters, let us offer our Lord the great and all-embracing sacrifice of our love, pouring out our treasury of hymns and prayers before him who offered his cross in sacrifice to God for the enrichment of us all.

Prayer

O GOD, who on this day,
through your Only Begotten Son,
have conquered death
and unlocked for us the path to eternity,
grant, we pray, that we who keep
the solemnity of the Lord's Resurrection
may, through the renewal brought by your Spirit,
rise up in the light of life.
Through our Lord Jesus Christ, your Son,
who lives and reigns with you in the unity of the Holy Spirit,
God, for ever and ever.

(Collect, Easter Sunday)

Jesus' final instruction and ascension

Acts 1: 1-11

DEAR Theophilus: In my previous book, Theophilus, I wrote of everything that Jesus did and taught from the beginning until the day he was taken up, after first giving instructions through the Holy Spirit to the apostles whom he had chosen.

After his passion Jesus had presented himself alive to them by many proofs. He appeared to them during forty days and spoke to them about the kingdom of God. When they were gathered together, he ordered them not to leave Jerusalem, saying, "Wait there for the promise of the Father about which you have heard me speak. For John baptized with water, but within a few days you will be baptized with the Holy Spirit."

As they were all gathered together, they asked him, "Lord, is this the time when you are going to restore the kingdom to Israel?" He replied, "It is not for you to know the dates or the times that the Father has designated by his own authority. But you will receive power when the Holy Spirit comes upon you, and then you will be my witnesses not only in Jerusalem, but throughout Judea and Samaria, and indeed to the farthest ends of the earth."

After he said this, he was lifted up as they looked on, and a cloud took him from their sight. While he was departing as they gazed upward toward the sky, suddenly two men dressed in white robes stood beside them, and they said, "Men of Galilee, why are you standing there looking up into the sky? This Jesus who has been taken up from you into heaven will come back in the same way as you have seen him going into heaven."

No one has ever ascended into heaven except the one who descended from heaven

Augustine: *Sermon*

TODAY our Lord Jesus Christ ascended into heaven; let our hearts ascend with him. Listen to the words of the Apostle: *If you have risen with Christ, set your hearts on the things that are above where Christ is, seated at the right hand of God; seek the things that are above, not the things that are on earth.* For just as he remained with us even after his ascension, so we too are already in heaven with him, even though what is promised us has not yet been fulfilled in our bodies.

Christ is now exalted above the heavens, but he still suffers on earth all the pain that we, the members of his body, have to bear. He showed this when he cried out from above: *Saul, Saul, why do you persecute me?* and when he said: *I was hungry and you gave me food.*

Why do we on earth not strive to find rest with him in heaven even now, through the faith, hope and love that unites us to him? While in heaven he is also with us; and we while on earth are with him. He is here with us by his divinity, his power and his love. We cannot be in heaven, as he is on earth, by divinity, but in him, we can be there by love.

He did not leave heaven when he came down to us; nor did he withdraw from us when he went up again into heaven. The fact that he was in heaven even while he was on earth is borne out by his own statement: *No one has ever ascended into heaven except the one who descended from heaven, the Son of Man, who is in heaven.*

Prayer

GRANT, we pray, almighty God,
that we, who believe that your Only Begotten Son, our Redeemer,
ascended this day to the heavens,
may in spirit dwell already in heavenly realms.
Who lives and reigns with you in the unity of the Holy Spirit,
God, for ever and ever.

(Collect, Ascension of the Lord, Mass during the Day)

PENTECOST

Jesus' appearance to the disciples

John 20:19-23

ON THE evening of that same day, the first day of the week, the doors of the house where the disciples had gathered were locked because of their fear of the Jews. Jesus then came and stood in their midst and said to them, "Peace be with you." After saying this, he showed them his hands and his side.

The disciples were filled with joy when they saw the Lord. "Peace be with you," Jesus said to them again. "As the Father has sent me, so I send you." After saying this, he breathed on them and said, "Receive the Holy Spirit. If you forgive anyone's sins, they are forgiven. If you retain anyone's sins, they are retained."

The sending of the Holy Spirit

Irenaeus: *Against Heresies*

WHEN the Lord told his disciples *to go and teach all nations and to baptize them in the name of the Father and of the Son and of the Holy Spirit,* he conferred on them the power of giving men new life in God.

He had promised through the prophets that in these last days he would pour out his Spirit on his servants and handmaids, and that they would prophesy. So when the Son of God became the Son of Man, the Spirit also descended upon him, becoming accustomed in this way to dwelling with the human race, to living in men and to inhabiting God's creation. The Spirit accomplished the Father's will in men who had grown old in sin, and gave them new life in Christ.

Luke says that the Spirit came down on the disciples at Pentecost, after the Lord's ascension, with power to open the gates of life to all nations and to make known to them the new covenant. So it was that men of every language joined in singing one song of praise to God, and scattered tribes, restored to unity by the Spirit, were offered to the Father as the firstfruits of all the nations.

This was why the Lord had promised to send the Advocate: he was to prepare us as an offering to God. Like dry flour, which cannot become one lump of dough, one loaf of bread, without moisture, we who are many could not become one in Christ Jesus without the water that comes down from heaven. And like parched ground, which yields no harvest unless it receives moisture, we who were once like a waterless tree could never have lived and borne fruit without this abundant rainfall from above. Through the baptism that liberates us from change and decay we have become one in body; through the Spirit we have become one in soul.

The Spirit of wisdom and understanding, the Spirit of counsel and strength, the Spirit of knowledge and the fear of God came down upon the Lord, and the Lord in turn gave this Spirit to his Church, sending the Advocate from heaven into all the world into which, according to his own words, the devil too had been cast down like lightning.

If we are not to be scorched and made unfruitful, we need the dew of God. Since we have our accuser, we need an Advocate as well. And so the Lord in his pity for man, who had fallen into the hands of brigands, having himself bound up his wounds and left for his care two coins bearing the royal image, entrusted him to the Holy Spirit. Now, through the Spirit, the image and inscription of the Father and the Son have been given to us, and it is our duty to use the coin committed to our charge and make it yield a rich profit for the Lord.

Prayer

O GOD, who by the mystery of today's great feast
sanctify your whole Church in every people and nation,
pour out, we pray, the gifts of the Holy Spirit
across the face of the earth
and, with the divine grace that was at work
when the Gospel was first proclaimed,
fill now once more the hearts of believers.

**Through our Lord Jesus Christ, your Son,
who lives and reigns with you in the unity of the Holy Spirit,
God, for ever and ever.**

(Collect, Pentecost, Mass during the Day)

Come Holy Spirit

Leader: Come Holy Spirit.

ALL: Fill the hearts of your faithful and kindle in them the fire of your love.

Leader: Send forth your Spirit and they shall be created.

ALL: And you shall renew the face of the earth.

Leader: O God, you taught the hearts of the faithful by the light of the Holy Spirit. Grant that, by the same Holy Spirit, we may be truly wise in what is right, and ever rejoice in his consolation. Through Christ our Lord.

ALL: Amen.

As morning breaks I look to you, O God, to be my strength this day, Alleluia.

MOST HOLY TRINITY

Commission of the apostles

Matthew 28:16-20

THE eleven disciples set out for Galilee, to the mountain where Jesus had told them to meet him. When they saw him, they prostrated themselves before him, although some doubted. Then Jesus approached them and said, "All authority in heaven and on earth has been given to me. Go, therefore, and make disciples of all nations, baptizing them in the name of the Father and of the Son and of the Holy Spirit, and teaching them to observe all that I have commanded you. And behold, I am with you always, to the end of the world."

I tasted and I saw

Catherine of Siena: *Dialogue*

ETERNAL God, eternal Trinity, you have made the blood of Christ so precious through his sharing in your divine nature. You are a mystery as deep as the sea; the more I search, the more I find, and the more I find, the more I search for you. But I can never be satisfied; what I receive will ever leave me desiring more.

When you fill my soul I have an even greater hunger, and I grow more famished for your light. I desire above all to see you, the true light, as you really are.

I have tasted and seen the depth of your mystery and the beauty of your creation with the light of my understanding. I have clothed myself with your likeness and have seen what I shall be.

Eternal Father, you have given me a share in your power and the wisdom that Christ claims as his own, and your Holy Spirit has given me the desire to love you. You are my Creator, eternal Trinity, and I am your creature. You have made of me a new creation in the blood of your Son, and I know that you are moved with love at the beauty of your creation, for you have enlightened me.

Eternal Trinity, Godhead, mystery deep as the sea, you could give me no greater gift than the gift of yourself. For you are a fire ever burning and never consumed, which itself consumes all the selfish love that fills my being. Yes, you are a fire that takes away the coldness, illuminates the mind with its light and causes me to know your truth.

By this light, reflected as it were in a mirror, I recognize that you are the highest good, one we can neither comprehend nor fathom. And I know that you are beauty and wisdom itself. The food of angels, you gave yourself to man in the fire of your love.

You are the garment which covers our nakedness, and in our hunger you are a satisfying food, for you are sweetness and in you there is no taste of bitterness, O triune God!

Prayer

GOD our Father, who by sending into the world the Word of truth and the Spirit of sanctification
made known to the human race your wondrous mystery,
grant us, we pray, that in professing the true faith,
we may acknowledge the Trinity of eternal glory
and adore your Unity, powerful in majesty.
Through our Lord Jesus Christ, your Son,
who lives and reigns with you in the unity of the Holy Spirit,
God, for ever and ever.

(Collect, Most Holy Trinity)

READINGS, PRAYERS, AND DEVOTIONS IN HONOR OF THE HOLY EUCHARIST

The mystery of faith

Paul VI: *Address of March 28, 1970.*

IS THE sacrament of the Eucharist hard to understand? Yes, it is hard, because it is a matter of something real and most unique which is accomplished by the divine power and which surpasses our normal natural capacity to comprehend. We have to believe it, on Christ's word; it is "the mystery of faith" par excellence.

But, let us be careful. In this sacrament the Lord presents himself to us not as he is but as he wishes us to consider him, as he wishes us to approach him. He offers himself to us under the aspect of expressive signs which he himself chose. It is as if he said: Look at me in this way, get to know me like this. The signs of the bread and wine are to tell you what I wish to be for you. He speaks to us by means of these signs, and says: This is how I am among you now.

Therefore, though we cannot enjoy his tangible presence, we can and ought to enjoy his real presence, under these significant forms. What is Jesus' intention in giving himself to us in the Eucharist? If we think about it well, we shall see that his intention is most patent! It tells us many, many things about Jesus. Above all, it tells us about his love. It tells us that he, Jesus, though he conceals himself in the Eucharist, also reveals himself in it, reveals himself in love. The "mystery of faith" opens up as the "mystery of love." Think of it: this is the sacramental garb which at the same time hides and reveals Jesus: bread and wine, given for us.

Jesus gives himself; presents himself. This is the center, the focal point of the whole of the gospel, of the Incarnation, of the Redemption. . . Born for us, given for us.

For each of us? Yes, for each of us. Jesus has multiplied his real but sacramental presence in time and number, in order to be able to offer each of us—we mean each of us—the good fortune, the joy to approach him, and to be able to say: He is for me, he is mine. "[He] loved me," St. Paul says, "and gave himself for me" (Gal 2:20).

And for all, too? Yes, for all. This is another aspect of Jesus' love which is expressed in the Eucharist. You know the words with which Jesus instituted this sacrament and which the priest repeats in the consecration at Mass: "eat, *all* of you; drink, *all of you* . . . ." For this same sacrament was instituted during an evening meal, a familiar and ordinary occasion and means of coming together, of being united. The Eucharist is the sacrament which represents and produces the unity of

Christians. This aspect of it is very dear to the Church and is highly valued today.

For example, the recent Council used the following extremely meaningful words about it: Christ "instituted in his Church the wonderful sacrament of the Eucharist by which the unity of the Church is both signified and effected."

Offering ourselves in union with Christ to the Father

Columba Marmion: *Christ the Life of the Soul*, pp. 256-257

WE MUST be united to Christ in his immolation and offer ourselves with him; then he takes us with him, he immolates us with him, he bears us before his Father, in the odor of sweetness. It is ourselves we must offer with Jesus Christ. If the faithful share, through baptism, in the priesthood of Christ, it is, says St. Peter, that they may "offer up spiritual sacrifices, acceptable to God through Jesus Christ" (1 Pt 2:5).

This is so true that in more than one prayer following the offering about to be made to God, the Church, while awaiting the moment of the consecration, lays stress on this union of our sacrifice with that of her Bridegroom. "Vouchsafe, O Lord," she says, "to sanctify these gifts, and receiving the oblation of this spiritual victim, make *us* an eternal sacrifice to yourself."

But in order for us to be thus accepted by God, the offering of ourselves must be united to the offering Christ made of himself upon the cross and renews upon the altar. Our Lord substituted himself for us in his immolation, he took the place of us all, and that is why when he died we, in principle, died with him: "Since one died for all, therefore all died" (2 Cor 5:14). For this mystical death to take place effectually in each one of us, we must unite ourselves to his sacrifice on the altar.

And how are we to unite ourselves to Christ Jesus in this character of victim? By yielding ourselves, like him, to the entire accomplishment of the divine good pleasure.

It is for God to fully dispose of the victim offered to him; we must be in this essential attitude of giving all to God, of making our acts of self-renunciation and mortification, of accepting the sufferings and trials of each day for love of him, so that we may be able to say, like Jesus Christ at the moment of his Passion: "I do this, that the world may know that I love the Father" (Jn 14:31)—that is, to offer ourselves with Jesus.

Let us offer the divine Son of his eternal Father and offer ourselves with this "holy Host" in the same dispositions that animated the Sacred Heart of Christ upon the cross: intense love of his Father and of our brethren, ardent desire for the salvation of souls, and full abandonment to all that is willed from on high, above all, if it contains what is painful and vexatious for our nature. When we do this, we offer God the most acceptable homage he can receive from us.

We herein have also the most certain means of being transformed into Jesus, especially if we unite ourselves to him in Communion, which is the most fruitful partaking of the Sacrifice of the Altar; for, if we are united to Christ he immolates us with him, renders us pleasing to his Father and makes us, by his grace, more and more like to himself.

Benediction of the Blessed Sacrament

O SAVING Victim, open wide
The gates of heaven to us below.
Our foes press on from every side.
Your aid supply, your strength bestow.
To your great name be endless praise,
Immortal Godhead, One in Three.
O grant us endless length of days
in our true native land with thee.
Amen.

Prayer at Benediction

(Congregation says verses marked 1; leader says scripture marked 2)

1. Lord, you have loved me from all eternity: therefore you created me.

2. Behold you are precious in my eyes and glorious because I love you (Isaiah 43:4).

1. You loved me after you created me: therefore you became man for me.

2. For God so loved the world that he gave his only begotten Son (John 3:16).

1. You loved me after you became man for me: therefore you lived and died for me.

2. Christ loved me and gave himself for me (Galatians 2:20).

1. You loved me after you died for me: therefore you rose from the grave for me.

2. I arose and I am still with you: even to the end of the world (Psalm 138—Matthew 28:20).

1. You loved me after you rose for me: therefore you went to prepare a place for me.

2. 1 am going to prepare a place for you that, where I am, you also may be (John 14:3).

l. You loved me after you had gone to prepare a place for me: therefore you came back to me.

O Jesus, you love me and want to live in me and be one with me. You become my very food and drink.

2. Take and eat—this is my body given for you.

Take and drink—this is my blood poured out for you (Luke 22:19).

l. This is the mystery on our altar, the mystery of your Blessed Sacrament, the mystery of your unspeakable love.

2. O if only you knew the gift of God! (John 4:10).

1. My song is love unknown: My Savior's love to me.

Love to the loveless shown, That I may lovely be.

2. This is my commandment: love one another even as I have loved you (John 15:12).

The following or another Eucharistic hymn is sung:

Humbly let us voice our homage
for so great a Sacrament.
Let all former rites surrender
to the Lord's new testament.
What our senses fail to fathom
let us grasp through faith's consent.
To the everlasting Father,
and the Son who reigns on high
with the Spirit blessed proceeding
forth from each eternally
Be salvation, honor, blessing,
might and endless majesty.
Amen.

The Divine Praises

Blessed be God.
Blessed be his holy name.
Blessed be Jesus Christ, true God and true man.
Blessed be the name of Jesus.
Blessed be his most sacred heart.
Blessed be his most precious blood.
Blessed be Jesus in the most holy sacrament of the altar.
Blessed be the Holy Spirit, the Comforter.
Blessed be the great Mother of God, Mary most holy.
Blessed be her holy and immaculate conception.
Blessed be her glorious assumption.
Blessed be the name of Mary, virgin and mother.
Blessed be St. Joseph, her most chaste spouse.
Blessed be God in his angels and in his saints.

Visit to the Blessed Sacrament

St. Alphonsus

MY LORD Jesus Christ, out of love for us all, you stay night and day in this Sacrament, full of compassion and love, waiting for, calling and welcoming all who come to visit you.

I believe that you are here in the Sacrament of the Altar. I adore you out of my nothingness. I thank you for all the graces you have bestowed on me—especially for having given me yourself in this sacrament, Mother Mary as my advocate, and for having called me to visit you in this church.

I now salute your most loving Heart to thank you for this great gift, to make up for all the outrages you face in this Sacrament and to adore you by this visit in every place where you are shunned and abandoned in this Sacrament.

My Jesus, I love you with all my heart. I am sorry for having so often offended your infinite goodness. Never let me offend you again.

I give everything to you—my will, my affections, my desires and all that I possess. From now on do whatever you want with me and all I have. All I ask for and want is your holy love, final perseverance and the perfect accomplishment of your will. I recommend to you the souls in Purgatory and all poor sinners.

Finally, my dear Savior, I unite all my affections with those of your most loving heart. I offer them all together to your Eternal Father. In your Name and for your love, may he accept and grant them.

The Morning Offering

O JESUS, through the immaculate Heart of Mary, I offer you all my prayers, works, joys, and sufferings of this day for all the intentions of your Sacred Heart, in union with the Holy Sacrifice of the Mass throughout the world, in reparation for my sins and in particular for this special intention.

“O Mary, . . . you are the glory of Jerusalem, the joy of Israel, the honor of our people.”

READINGS AND PRAYERS IN HONOR OF MARY, THE MOTHER OF GOD

In praise of Mary, Mother of God

Cyrus of Alexandria: *Homily*

MARY, Mother of God, we salute you. Precious vessel worthy of the whole world's reverence, you are an ever-shining light, the crown of virginity, the symbol of orthodoxy, an indestructible temple, the place that held him whom no place can contain, mother and virgin. Because of you the holy gospels could say: *Blessed is he who comes in the name of the Lord.*

We salute you, for in your holy womb was confined him who is beyond all limitation. Because of you the holy Trinity is glorified and adored; the cross is called precious and is venerated throughout the world; the heavens exult; the angels and archangels make merry; demons are put to flight; the devil, that tempter, is thrust down from heaven; the fallen race of man is taken up on high; all creatures possessed by the madness of idolatry have attained knowledge of the truth; believers receive holy baptism; the oil of gladness is poured out; the Church is established throughout the world, pagans are brought to repentance.

What more is there to say? Because of you the light of the only-begotten Son of God has shone upon those who sat in darkness and in the shadow of death; prophets pronounced the word of God; the apostles preached salvation to the Gentiles;

the dead are raised to life, and kings rule by the power of the holy Trinity.

Who can put Mary's high honor into words? She is both mother and virgin. I am overwhelmed by the wonder of this miracle.

PRAYERS TO OUR LADY

The Memorare

REMEMBER, O most gracious Virgin Mary, that never was it known that anyone who fled to your protection, implored your help, or sought your intercession, was left unaided. Inspired by this confidence, I fly unto you, O Virgin of virgins, my Mother. To you do I come; before you I stand, sinful and sorrowful. O Mother of the Word Incarnate, despise not my petitions, but in your mercy, hear and answer me. Amen.

Hail Holy Queen

HAIL, holy Queen, mother of mercy, our life, our sweetness and our hope. To you do we cry, poor banished children of Eve. To you do we send up our sighs, mourning and weeping in this valley of tears. Turn then, most gracious advocate, your eyes of mercy towards us; and after this our exile show unto us the blessed fruit of your womb, Jesus. O clement, O loving, O sweet Virgin Mary.

We Fly to Your Patronage
(Sub tuum praesidium)

WE FLY to your patronage, O holy Mother of God; despise not our petition in our necessities, but deliver us always from all dangers, O glorious and blessed Virgin.

To Mary Immaculate

YOU are all fair, O Mary, and the original stain was never in you. You are the glory of Jerusalem, the joy of Israel, the honor of our people. You are the advocate of sinners, O Mary, Virgin most prudent, Mother most merciful; please pray for us. Intercede for us with our Lord Jesus, your Son. Amen.

Holy Mary, Help the Helpless

HOLY Mary, help the helpless, strengthen the fearful, comfort the sorrowful, pray for the people, plead for the clergy, intercede for all women consecrated to God; may all who keep your sacred commemoration experience the might of your assistance. Amen.

Visit to Mary by St. Alphonsus

MOST Holy Immaculate Virgin and my mother Mary, to you who are the mother of my Lord, the Queen of the world, the advocate, the hope, the refuge of sinners, I have recourse today. I, who am the most miserable of all. I offer you my most humble homage, O great Queen, and I thank you for all the graces you have conferred on me until now, particularly for having preserved me by your prayers.

I love you, O most amiable Lady; and because of the love I have for you, I promise to serve you always and to do all I can to make others love you. I place in you all my hopes. I confide my salvation to your care. Accept me for your servant and receive me under your mantle, O mother of mercy. And since you are so powerful with God, deliver me from all temptations, or rather obtain for me the strength to triumph over them until death.

Of you I ask a perfect love for Jesus Christ. From you I hope to die a good death. O my mother, by the love which you have for God, I beseech you to help me at all times, but especially at the last moment of my life. Leave me not, I beseech you, until you see me safe in heaven, blessing you and singing your mercies for all eternity. Amen.

Prayer to Our Lady of Fatima

O MOST holy Virgin Mary, Queen of the most holy Rosary, you were pleased to appear to the children of Fatima and reveal a glorious message. We implore you, inspire in our hearts a fervent love for the recitation of the Rosary. By meditating on the mysteries of the redemption that are recalled therein may we obtain the graces and virtues that we ask, through the merits of Jesus Christ, our Lord and Redeemer.

Prayer to Our Lady of Good Counsel

MOST glorious Virgin, you were chosen by the eternal Counsel to be the Mother of the eternal Word made flesh. You are the treasurer of divine graces and the advocate of sinners. I who am your most unworthy servant have recourse to you. Graciously be my guide and counselor in this valley of tears.

Obtain for me, through the Precious Blood of your divine Son, the forgiveness of my sins, the salvation of my soul, and the means necessary to obtain it. In like manner, obtain for holy Church victory over her enemies and the spread of Jesus' kingdom over the whole earth.

Prayer to Our Lady of Guadalupe

OUR Lady of Guadalupe, mystical rose, intercede for the Church, protect the holy Father, help all who invoke you in their necessities. Since you are the ever Virgin Mary and Mother of the true God, obtain for us from your most holy Son the grace of a firm and a sure hope amid the bitterness of life, as well as an ardent love and the precious gift of final perseverance.

Prayer to Our Lady, Help of Christians

MARY, powerful Virgin, you are the mighty and glorious protector of the Church. You are the marvelous help of Christians. You are awe-inspiring as an army in battle array. In the midst of our anguish, struggle, and distress, defend us from the power of the enemy, and at the hour of our death receive our soul in heaven.

Prayer to Our Lady of Lourdes

O IMMACULATE Virgin Mary, you are the refuge of sinners, the health of the sick, and the comfort of the afflicted. By your appearances at the Grotto of Lourdes you made it a privileged sanctuary where your favors are given to people streaming to it from the whole world. Over the years countless sufferers have obtained the cure of their infirmities whether of soul, mind, or body. Therefore I come with limitless confidence to implore your motherly intercession.

THE ROSARY

IN THE name of the Father and of the Son and of the Holy Spirit. Amen.

I believe in God, the Father almighty, Creator of heaven and earth, and in Jesus Christ, his only Son, our Lord, who was conceived by the Holy Spirit, born of the Virgin Mary, suffered under Pontius Pilate, was crucified, died and was buried; he descended into hell; on the third day he rose again from the dead; he ascended into heaven, and is seated at the right hand of God the Father almighty; from there he will come to judge the living and the dead. I believe in the Holy Spirit, the holy catholic Church, the communion of Saints, the forgiveness of sins, the resurrection of the body and life everlasting. Amen.

Our Father, who art in heaven, hallowed be thy name; thy kingdom come, thy will be done on earth as it is in heaven. Give us this day our daily bread, and forgive us our trespasses, as we forgive those who trespass against us; and lead us not into temptation, but deliver us from evil. Amen.

Hail Mary, full of grace, the Lord is with thee, blessed art thou among women and blessed is the fruit of thy womb, Jesus. Holy Mary, Mother of God, pray for us sinners now and at the hour of our death. Amen . . . (three times)

Glory to the Father, and to the Son, and to the Holy Spirit, as it was in the beginning, is now and will be for ever. Amen.

The Joyful Mysteries

(For Mondays and Saturdays
from Advent until Lent)

The First Mystery

Leader: The Annunciation—The angel Gabriel proclaims to Mary of Nazareth that she will give birth to Jesus, eternal Son of God and Savior of our race. Mary accepts her destiny: "I am the servant of the Lord. Let it be done to me according to your word" (Luke 1:38).

Let us offer this decade for the Church throughout the world, but especially for our holy father, the Pope, and all the Bishops of the United States.

The Second Mystery

Leader: The Visitation—Mary leaves Nazareth to be with her cousin Elizabeth, soon to give birth to John the Baptist. Elizabeth greets her with the words: "Blessed are you among women, and blessed is the fruit of your womb. And why am I so greatly favored that the mother of my Lord should visit me?" (Luke 1:42-43).

Let us offer this decade for all the departed, especially for our relatives, our friends, and the deceased members of our group.

The Third Mystery

Leader: The Nativity—Mary and Joseph arrive in Bethlehem. There Mary gave birth to Jesus, wrapped him in swaddling clothes and laid him in a manger because there was no room for them in the place where travelers stayed.

Let us offer this decade for our families, for our wives (our husbands), our children, and all our relatives.

The Fourth Mystery

Leader: The Presentation of Jesus in the Temple—Simeon warns Mary: "This child is destined for the fall and the rise of many in Israel, and to be a sign that will be opposed, so that the secret thoughts of many will be revealed, and you yourself a sword will pierce" (Luke 2:34-35).

Let us offer this decade for the sick, the homeless, for those suffering mental illness and for those now on their death bed.

The Fifth Mystery

Leader: The Finding in the Temple—The twelve year old Jesus was missing for three days. When Mary and Joseph finally found him in the temple, he said to them: "Why were you searching for me? Did you not know that I must be in my Father's house?" (Luke 2:49).

Let us offer this decade for the intention nearest to our heart.

The Luminous Mysteries*

(For Thursdays except during Lent)

The First Mystery

Leader: The Baptism of Jesus—Christ was baptized by John the Baptist in the Jordan River. At that time, the Father called him his beloved Son and

*Added to the Mysteries of the Rosary by Pope John Paul II in his Apostolic Letter of October 16, 2002, entitled *The Rosary of the Virgin Mary.* They are reprinted here from our book *St. Joseph Sunday Missal for 2005,* which in 2004 received the Imprimatur from Most Rev. Frank J. Rodimer, Bishop of Paterson.

the Holy Spirit descended on him to invest him with the mission he was to carry out.

Let us offer this decade for the Church throughout the world, but especially for our holy father, the Pope, and all the Bishops of the United States.

The Second Mystery

Leader: Christ's Self-Manifestation at Cana—Christ manifested himself at the wedding in Cana. He changed water into wine and opened the hearts of the disciples to faith, thanks to the intervention of Mary, the first among believers.

Let us offer this decade for all the departed, especially for our relatives, our friends, and the deceased members of our group.

The Third Mystery

Leader: Christ's Proclamation of the Kingdom—Christ proclaimed the Kingdom of God (by means of its Magna Carta, the Sermon on the Mount, and especially the Beatitudes), and its call to forgiveness as he inaugurated the ministry of mercy, which he continues to exercise until the end of the world, particularly through the Sacrament of Reconciliation.

Let us offer this decade for our families, for our wives (our husbands), our children, and all our relatives.

The Fourth Mystery

Leader: The Transfiguration—Christ was transfigured in the presence of Sts. Peter, John and James. The glory of the Godhead shone forth from his face as the Father commanded the Apostles to listen to him and experience his Passion and Resurrection and be transfigured by the Holy Spirit.

Let us offer this decade for the sick, the homeless, for those suffering mental illness and for those now on their death bed.

The Fifth Mystery

Leader: Christ's Institution of the Eucharist—Christ instituted the Eucharist at the Last Supper. He offered his Body and Blood as food under the signs of bread and wine and testified to his love for humanity, for whose sake he would offer himself in sacrifice.

Let us offer this decade for the intention nearest to our heart.

The Sorrowful Mysteries

(For Tuesdays and Fridays and daily from Ash Wednesday until Easter Sunday)

The First Mystery

Leader: The Agony in the Garden—Jesus went down on his knees and prayed: "Father, if you are willing, take this cup from me. Yet not my will but yours be done. . ." In his anguish, he prayed so fervently that his sweat became like great drops of blood falling on the ground (Luke 22:42-44).

Let us offer this decade for the Church throughout the world, but especially for our holy father, the Pope, and all the Bishops of the United States.

The Second Mystery

Leader: The Scourging—Pilate's next move was to have Jesus scourged. Isaiah says: "Without beauty, without majesty, we saw him, a thing despised and rejected by men and women, a man of sorrows and familiar with suffering" (Is. 53:2-3).

Let us offer this decade for all the departed, especially for our relatives, our friends, and the deceased members of our group.

The Third Mystery

Leader: The Crowning with Thorns—The soldiers then wove a crown of thorns and fixed it on his head, throwing around his shoulders a cloak of royal purple. Repeatedly they came up to him and said, "All hail, king of the Jews!" slapping his face as they did so (John 19:1-2).

Let us offer this decade for our families, for our wives (our husbands), our children, and all our relatives.

The Fourth Mystery

Leader: The Carrying of the Cross—And yet ours were the sufferings he bore, ours the sorrows he carried. . . . We had all gone astray like sheep, each taking his own way, and God burdened him with the sins of all of us (Is. 53:4-6).

Let us offer this decade for the sick, the homeless, for those suffering mental illness and for those now on their death bed.

The Fifth Mystery

Leader: The Crucifixion—He was pierced through for our offenses, crushed for our sins. On him lies the punishment that brings us peace, and through his wounds we are healed (Is. 53:5).

Let us offer this decade for the intention nearest to our heart.

The Glorious Mysteries

(Wednesdays [except during Lent] and Sundays from Easter until Advent)

The First Mystery

Leader: The Resurrection—On the evening of the first day of the week, even though the disciples had locked the doors of the place where they were for fear of the Jews, Jesus came and stood before them. "Peace be with you," he said. When he had said this, he showed them his hands and his side. At the sight of the Lord, the disciples rejoiced (John 20:19-20).

Let us offer this decade for the Church throughout the world, but especially for our holy father, the Pope, and all the Bishops of the United States.

The Second Mystery

Leader: The Ascension—The eleven disciples set out for Galilee, to the mountain where Jesus had told them to meet him . . . Jesus came near to them and said. "All authority in heaven and on earth has been given to me. Go, therefore, and make disciples of all nations, baptizing them in the name of the Father and of the Son and of the Holy Spirit, and teaching them to observe all that I have commanded you. And behold, I am with you always, to the end of the world" (Matthew 28:16-20).

Let us offer this decade for all the departed, especially for our relatives, our friends, and the deceased members of our group.

The Third Mystery

Leader: Descent of the Holy Spirit—When the day of Pentecost came it found them gathered in one place. Suddenly from up in the sky there came a noise like a strong, driving wind which was heard all through the house where they were seated. Tongues of fire appeared which parted and came to rest on each of them. All were filled with the Holy Spirit (Acts 2:1-4).

Let us offer this decade for our families, for our wives (our husbands), our children, and all our relatives.

The Fourth Mystery

Leader: The Assumption of Mary—Mary had said: "My soul proclaims the greatness of the Lord and my spirit rejoices in God my Savior. For he has looked with favor on the lowliness of his servant; henceforth all generations will call me blessed. The Mighty One has done great things for me, and holy is his name" (Luke 1:46-49).

How blessed you are, Mary ever virgin. You have left this world to be joined with your son, Jesus Christ. Graced by his power, you shine forth like the sun among the saints.

Let us offer this decade for the sick, the homeless, for those suffering mental illness and for those now on their death bed.

The Fifth Mystery

Leader: Crowning of Mary as Queen of Heaven—A great sign appeared in heaven: a woman clothed with the sun, with the moon beneath her feet, and a crown of twelve stars on her head (Rev. 12:1).

Let us offer this decade for the intention nearest to our heart.

Hail Holy Queen, etc.

Let us pray.

O GOD, whose only begotten Son, by his life, death and resurrection has purchased for us the rewards of eternal life, grant that while meditating upon these mysteries of the most holy Rosary of the Blessed Virgin Mary, we may both imitate what they contain and obtain what they promise, through the same Christ our Lord. Amen.

PRAYER SERVICE IN HONOR OF OUR MOTHER OF PERPETUAL HELP

Leader: Born of earth, yet called from heaven, Mary said "YES" to God. She gave birth to the Savior, raised him to greatness, and stood helpless as he died on the cross. Risen in glory, Jesus shares her with us. Beholding our Mother's strength, we too can say "YES" to God.

Opening Song

Leader: Let us pray: Almighty God, life is your most sacred gift. You implanted divine life in Mary and she gave birth to the Savior of the world. You share divine life with each of us and ask us to share your saving love with all those we meet. May we join Mary and say "YES" to all that you call us to be and to do. We ask this through Christ our Lord.

ALL: Amen.

First Reading

(PAUSE FOR SILENT REFLECTION)

Leader: Mary, you are the most perfect witness of the redemption. Aid us to be like you in living and announcing it to the world.

ALL: Mary, Our Mother of Perpetual Help, pray for us.

Leader: Mary, you are the new creation, the new beginning, because you manifest best your son's infinite grace and love.

ALL: Mary, Our Mother of Perpetual Help, pray for us.

Leader: Mary, by your Immaculate Conception, you are truly the principal patroness of our country. May you always watch over us and lead us to Christ.

ALL: Mary, Our Mother of Perpetual Help, pray for us.

Leader: Mary, you are the springtime of the new creation which Jesus began in the Passover.

ALL: Mary, Our Perpetual Help, pray for us.

Second Reading

(Taken from the *Visits to the Blessed Sacrament* by St. Alphonsus Liguori)

ALL: My Lady, St. Bernard calls you "the Ravisher of hearts." He says that you go about stealing hearts by the charms of your beauty and goodness. Steal also my heart and will, I beseech you. I give it wholly to you; offer it to God with your own.

Solemn incensation of the picture followed by silent reflection

Leader: Mary give us Jesus, the light of the world.

ALL: May he shine forth through our ministry to the poor and most abandoned.

Leader: Mary gives us Jesus Crucified.

ALL: By dying to our selfish inclinations may we give life to those we live with.

Leader: Mary gives us Jesus risen to new life.

ALL: May our life of sacrifice and service bring us new life in this world and the next.

Third Reading

(PAUSE FOR SILENT REFLECTION)

ALL: Remember, O Most Loving Virgin Mary, that never was it known that anyone who fled to your protection, or sought your help, was ever left unaided. Inspired by this confidence, we turn to you,

O Virgin of virgins, Our Mother. To you do we come. Before you we stand, sinful and sorrowful. O Mother of the Word Incarnate, do not despise our petitions, but in your mercy hear and answer us. Amen.

Closing Response

Leader: May Mary's pilgrimage of faith strengthen us in our vocations.

ALL: Amen.

Leader: May Mary's loving desire that her Son's words be heeded hasten the unity of all Christians in faith.

ALL: Amen.

Leader: May Mary's motherly intercession help us to become worthy of Jesus' promises.

ALL: Amen.

Leader: Mary is the daughter of God the Father, Spouse of God the Holy Spirit and Mother of God the Son. May the blessing of the Holy Trinity come upon us, who honor Mary, and remain with us forever.

ALL: Amen.

Closing Hymn

“We seek from the saints example in their way of life, fellowship in their communion, and aid by their intercession” (Vatican II).

READINGS AND PRAYERS FROM THE SAINTS AND SPIRITUAL WRITERS

READINGS

The song of the Church

Pius X: *Apostolic Constitution*

THE collection of psalms found in Scripture composed as it was under divine inspiration, has from the very beginnings of the Church, shown a wonderful power of fostering devotion among Christians as they offer *to God a continuous sacrifice of praise, the harvest of lips blessing his name.* Following a custom already established in the Old Law, the psalms have played a conspicuous part in the sacred liturgy itself, and in the divine office.

The psalms have also a wonderful power to awake in our hearts the desire for every virtue. Athanasius says: *Though all Scripture, both old and new, is divinely inspired and has its use in teaching, as we read in Scripture itself yet the*

Book of Psalms, like a garden enclosing the fruits of all the other books, produces their fruits in song, and in the process of singing brings forth its own special fruits to take their place beside them. In the same place Athanasius rightly adds: *The psalms seem to me to be like a mirror, in which the person using them can see himself, and the stirrings of his own heart; he can recite them against the background of his own emotions.* Augustine says in his Confessions: *How I wept when I heard your hymns and canticles, being deeply moved by the sweet singing of your Church. Those voices flowed into my ears, truth filtered into my heart, and from my heart surged waves of devotion. Tears ran down, and I was happy in my tears.*

Indeed, who could fail to be moved by those many passages in the psalms which set forth so profoundly the infinite majesty of God, his omnipotence, his justice and goodness and clemency, too deep for words, and all the other infinite qualities of his that deserve our praise? Who could fail to be roused to the same emotions by the prayers of thanksgiving to God for blessings received, by the petitions, so humble and confident, for blessings still awaited, by the cries of a soul in sorrow for sin committed? Who would not be fired with love as he looks on the likeness of Christ, the redeemer, here so lovingly foretold? His was *the voice* Augustine *heard in every psalm, the voice of praise, of suffering, of joyful expectation, of present distress.*

The glorious duty of man: to pray and to love

John Mary Vianney, *Catechetical instructions*

MY LITTLE children, reflect on these words: the Christian's treasure is not on earth but in heaven. Our thoughts, then, ought to be directed to where our treasure is. This is the glorious duty of man: to pray and to love. If you pray and love, that is where a man's happiness lies.

Prayer is nothing else but union with God. When one has a heart that is pure and united with God, he is given a kind of serenity and sweetness that makes him ecstatic, a light that surrounds him with marvelous brightness. In this intimate union, God and the soul are fused together like two bits of wax that no one can ever pull apart. This union of God with a tiny creature is a lovely thing. It is a happiness beyond understanding.

We had become unworthy to pray, but God in his goodness allowed us to speak with him. Our prayer is incense that gives him the greatest pleasure.

My little children, your hearts are small, but prayer stretches them and makes them capable of loving God. Through prayer we receive a foretaste of heaven and something of paradise comes down upon us. Prayer never leaves us without sweetness. It is honey that flows into the soul and makes all things sweet. When we pray properly, sorrows disappear like snow before the sun.

Your kingdom come

Teresa of Avila: *Way of Perfection*

WHEN asking a favor of some person of importance would anyone be so ill-mannered and thoughtless as not first to consider how best to address him in order to make a good impression and give him no cause for offense? Surely he would think over his petition carefully and his reason for making it, especially if it were for something specific and important as our good Jesus tells us our petitions should be. It seems to me that this point deserves serious attention. My Lord, could you not have included all in one word by saying: "Father, give us whatever is good for us"? After all, to one who understands everything so perfectly, what need is there to say more?

O Eternal Wisdom, between you and your Father that was enough; that was how you prayed in the garden. You expressed your desire and fear but surrendered yourself to his will. But as for us, my Lord, you know that we are less submissive to the will of your Father and need to mention each thing separately in order to stop and think whether it would be good for us, and otherwise not ask for it. You see, the gift our Lord intends for us may be by far the best, but if it is not what we wanted we are quite capable of flinging it back in his face. That is the kind of people we are; ready cash is the only wealth we understand.

Therefore, the good Jesus bids us repeat these words, this prayer for his kingdom to come in us:

Hallowed be your name, your kingdom come. See how wise our Master is! But what do we mean when we pray for this kingdom? That is what I am going to consider now, for it is important that we should understand it. Our good Jesus placed these two petitions side by side because he realized that in our inadequacy we could never fittingly hallow, praise, exalt or glorify this holy name of the eternal Father unless he enabled us to do so by giving us his kingdom here on earth. But since we must know what we are asking for and how important it is to pray for it without ceasing and to do everything in our power to please him who is to give it to us, I should now like to give you my own thoughts on the matter.

Of the many joys that are found in the kingdom of heaven, the greatest seems to me to be the sense of tranquility and well-being that we shall experience when we are free from all concern for earthly things. Glad because others are glad and for ever at peace, we shall have the deep satisfaction of seeing that by all creatures the Lord is honored and praised, and his name blessed.

No one ever offends him, for there everyone loves him. Loving him is the soul's one concern. Indeed it cannot help but love him, for it knows him. Here below our love must necessarily fall short of that perfection and constancy, but even so how different it would be, how much more like that of heaven, if we really knew our Lord!

Our daily work is to do the will of God

Elizabeth Seton: *Conference*

I WILL tell you what is my own great help. I once read or heard that an interior life means but the continuation of our Savior's life in us; that the great object of all his mysteries is to merit for us the grace of his interior life and communicate it to us, it being the end of his mission to lead us into the sweet land of promise, a life of constant union with himself.

And what was the first rule of our dear Savior's life? You know it was to do his Father's will. Well, then, the first end I propose in our daily work is to do the will of God; secondly, to do it in the manner he wills; and thirdly, to do it because it is his will.

I know what his will is by those who direct me; whatever they bid me do, if it is ever so small in itself, is the will of God for me. Then do it in the manner he wills it, not sewing an old thing as if it were new, or a new thing as if it were old; not fretting because the oven is too hot, or in a fuss because it is too cold. You understand—not flying and driving because you are hurried, not creeping like a snail because no one pushes you.

Our dear Savior was never in extremes. The third object is to do his will because God wills it, that is, to be ready to quit at any moment and to do anything else to which you may be called. . . .

You think it very hard to lead a life of such restraint unless you keep your eye of faith always open. Perseverance is a great grace. To go on gaining and advancing every day, we must be resolute, and bear and suffer as our blessed forerunners did. Which of them gained heaven without a struggle? . . .

What are our real trials? By what name shall we call them? One cuts herself out a cross of pride; another, one of causeless discontent; another, one of restless impatience or peevish fretfulness. But is the whole any better than children's play if looked at with the common eye of faith? Yet we know certainly that our God calls us to a holy life, that he gives every grace, every abundant grace; and though we are so weak of ourselves, this grace is able to carry us through every obstacle and difficulty.

But we lack courage to keep a continual watch over nature, and therefore, year after year, with our thousand graces, multiplied resolutions, and fair promises, we run around in a circle of misery and imperfections. After a long time in the service of God, we come nearly to the point from whence we set out, and perhaps with even less ardor for penance and mortification than when we began our consecration to him.

You are now in your first set out. Be above the vain fears of nature and efforts of your enemy. You are children of eternity. Your immortal crown awaits you, and the best of Fathers waits there to reward your duty and love. You may indeed sow here in tears, but you may be sure there to reap in joy.

Put Christ before everything

Benedict: *Rule*

WHENEVER you begin any good work you should first of all make a most pressing appeal to Christ our Lord to bring it to perfection; that he, who has honored us by counting us among his children, may never be grieved by our evil deeds. For we must always serve him with the good things he has given us in such a way that he may never—as an angry father disinherits his sons or even like a master who inspires fear—grow impatient with our sins and consign us to everlasting punishment, like wicked servants who would not follow him to glory.

So we should at long last rouse ourselves, prompted by the words of Scripture: *Now is the time for us to rise from sleep.* Our eyes should be open to the God-given light, and we should listen in wonderment to the message of the divine voice as it daily cries out: *Today, if you shall hear his voice, harden not your hearts;* and again: *If anyone has ears to hear, let him listen to what the Spirit is saying to the churches.* And what does the Spirit say? *Come my sons, listen to me; I will teach you the fear of the Lord. Hurry, while you have the light of life, so that death's darkness may not overtake you.*

On the love of Christ

Alphonsus Liguori: *Sermon*

ALL holiness and perfection of soul lies in our love for Jesus Christ our God, who is our redeemer and our supreme good. It is part of the love of God to acquire and to nurture all the virtues which make a man perfect.

Has not God in fact won for himself a claim on all our love? From all eternity he has loved us. And it is in this vein that he speaks to us: "O man, consider carefully that I first loved you. You had not yet appeared in the light of day, nor did the world yet exist, but already I loved you. From all eternity I have loved you."

Since God knew that man is enticed by favors, he wished to bind him to his love by means of his gifts: "I want to catch men with the snares, those chains of love in which they allow themselves to be entrapped, so that they will love me." And all the gifts which he bestowed on man were given to this end. He gave him a soul, made in his likeness, and endowed with memory, intellect and will; he gave him a body equipped with the senses; it was for him that he created heaven and earth and such an abundance of things. He made all these things out of love for man, so that all creation might serve man, and man in turn might love God out of gratitude for so many gifts.

But he did not wish to give us only beautiful creatures; the truth is that to win for himself our love, he went so far as to bestow upon us the fullness of himself. The eternal Father went so far as to give his Son. When he saw that we were all dead through sin and deprived of his grace, what did he do? Compelled, as the Apostle says, by the superabundance of his love for us, he sent his beloved Son to make reparation for us and to call us back to a sinless life.

By giving us his Son, whom he did not spare precisely so that he might spare us, he bestowed on us at once every good: grace, love and heaven; for all these goods are certainly inferior *to the Son. He who did not spare his own Son, but handed him over for all of us; how could he fail to give us along with his Son all good things?*

Serving the poor is to be our first preference

Vincent de Paul: *Letter*

EVEN though the poor are often rough and unrefined, we must not judge them from external appearances nor from the mental gifts they seem to have received. On the contrary, if you consider the poor in the light of faith, then you will observe that they are taking the place of the Son of God who chose to be poor. Although in his passion he almost lost the appearance of a man and was considered a fool by the Gentiles and a stumbling block by the Jews, he showed them that his mission was to preach to the poor: *He sent me to preach the good news to the poor.* We also ought to have this same spirit and imitate Christ's actions, that is, we must take care of the poor, console them, help them, support their cause.

We preach Christ crucified

Paul of the Cross: *Letter*

IT IS very good and holy to consider the passion of our Lord and to meditate on it, for by this sacred path we reach union with God. In this most holy school we learn true wisdom, for it was there that all the saints learned it. Indeed when the cross of our dear Jesus has planted its roots more deeply in your hearts, then will you rejoice: "To suffer and not to die," or, "Either to suffer or to die," or better: "Neither to suffer, nor to die, but only to turn perfectly to the will of God."

Love is a unifying virtue which takes upon itself the torments of its beloved Lord. It is a fire reaching through to the inmost soul. It transforms the lover into the one loved. More deeply, love intermingles with grief, and grief with love, and a certain blending of love and grief occurs. They become so united that we can no longer distinguish love from grief nor grief from love. Thus the loving heart rejoices in its sorrow and exults in its grieving love.

Therefore, be constant in practicing every virtue, and especially in imitating the patience of our dear Jesus, for this is the summit of pure love. Live in such a way that all may know that you bear outwardly as well as inwardly the image of Christ crucified, the model of all gentleness and mercy. For if a man is united inwardly with the Son of the living God, he also bears his likeness outwardly by his continual practice of heroic goodness, and especially through a patience reinforced by courage, which does not complain either secretly or in public. Conceal yourselves in Jesus crucified, and hope for nothing except that all men be thoroughly converted to his will.

When you become true lovers of the Crucified, you will always celebrate the feast of the cross in the inner temple of the soul, bearing all in silence and not relying on any creature. Since festivals ought to be celebrated joyfully, those who love the Crucified should honor the feast of the cross by enduring in silence with a serene and joyful countenance, so that their suffering remains hidden from men and is observed by God alone. For in this feast there is always a solemn banquet, and the food presented is the will of God, exemplified by the love of our crucified Christ.

Wherein sin abounded grace has overflowed

Bernard: *Sermon on the Song of Songs*

WHERE can the weak find a place of firm security and peace, except in the wounds of the Savior? Indeed, the more secure is my place there the more he can do to help me. The world rages, the flesh is heavy, and the devil lays his snares, but I do not fall, for my feet are planted on firm rock. I may have sinned gravely. My conscience would be distressed, but it would not be in turmoil, for I would recall the wounds of the Lord: *he was wounded for our iniquities.* What sin is there so deadly that it cannot be pardoned by the death of Christ? And so if I bear in mind this strong, effective remedy, I can never again be terrified by the malignancy of sin.

Surely the man who said, *My sin is too great to merit pardon,* was wrong. He was speaking as though he were not a member of Christ and had no share in his merits, so that he could claim them as his own, as a member of the body can claim what belongs to the head. As for me, what can I appropriate that I lack from the heart of the

Lord who abounds in mercy? They pierced his hands and feet and opened his side with a spear. Through the openings of these wounds I may drink *honey from the rock and oil from the hardest stone:* that is, I may *taste and see that the Lord is sweet.*

He was thinking thoughts of peace, and I did not know it, *for who knows the mind of the Lord, or who has been his counselor?* But the piercing nail has become a key to unlock the door, that I may see the good will of the Lord. And what can I see as I look through the hole? Both the nail and the wound cry out that God was in Christ reconciling the world to himself. *The sword pierced his soul and came close to his heart,* so that he might be able to feel compassion for me in my weaknesses.

Through these sacred wounds we can see the secret of his heart, the great mystery of love, *the sincerity of his mercy with which he visited us from on high.* Where have your love, your mercy, your compassion shone out more luminously than in your wounds, sweet, gentle Lord of mercy? More mercy than this no one has than that he lay down his life for those who are doomed to death.

The knowledge of the mystery hidden in Christ Jesus

John of the Cross: *Spiritual canticle*

THOUGH holy doctors have uncovered many mysteries and wonders, and devout souls have understood them in this earthly condition of ours, yet the greater part still remains to be unfolded by them, and even to be understood by them.

We must then dig deeply in Christ. He is like a rich mine with many pockets containing treasures: however deep we dig we will never find their end or their limit. Indeed, in every pocket new seams of fresh riches are discovered on all sides.

For this reason the apostle Paul said of Christ: *In him are hidden all the treasures of the wisdom and knowledge of God.* The soul cannot enter into these treasures, nor attain them, unless it first crosses into and enters the thicket of suffering, enduring interior and exterior labors, and unless it first receives from God very many blessings in the intellect and in the senses, and has undergone long spiritual training.

All these are lesser things, disposing the soul for the lofty sanctuary of the knowledge of the mysteries of Christ: this is the highest wisdom attainable in this life.

Would that men might come at last to see that it is quite impossible to reach the thicket of the riches and wisdom of God except by first entering the thicket of much suffering, in such a way that the soul finds there its consolation and desire. The soul that longs for divine wisdom chooses first, and in truth, to enter the thicket of the cross.

Saint Paul therefore urges the Ephesians *not to grow weary in the midst of tribulations*, but to be *rooted and grounded in love, so that they may know with all the saints the breadth, the length, the height and the depth—to know what is beyond knowledge, the love of Christ, so as to be filled with all the fullness of God.*

The gate that gives entry into these riches of his wisdom is the cross; because it is a narrow gate, while many seek the joys that can be gained through it, it is given to few to desire to pass through it.

She longed for Christ, though she thought he had been taken away

Gregory the Great: *Homily*

WHEN Mary Magdalene came to the tomb and did not find the Lord's body, she thought it had been taken away and so informed the disciples. After they came and saw the tomb, they too believed what Mary had told them. The text then says: *The disciples went back home,* and it adds: *but Mary wept and remained standing outside the tomb.*

We should reflect on Mary's attitude and the great love she felt for Christ; for though the disciples had left the tomb, she remained. She was still seeking the one she had not found, and while she sought she wept; burning with the fire of love, she longed for him who she thought had been taken away. And so it happened that the woman who stayed behind to seek Christ was the only one to see him. For perseverance is essential to any good deed, as the voice of truth tells us: *Whoever perseveres to the end will be saved.*

At first she sought but did not find, but when she persevered it happened that she found what she was looking for. When our desires are not satisfied, they grow stronger, and becoming stronger they take hold of their object. Holy desires likewise grow with anticipation, and if they do not grow they are not really desires. Anyone who succeeds in attaining the truth has burned with such a love. As David says: *My soul has thirsted for the living God; when shall I come and appear before the face of God?* And so also in the Song of Songs the Church says: *I was wounded by love;* and again: *My soul is melted with love.*

Woman, why are you weeping? Whom do you seek? She is asked why she is sorrowing so that her desire might be strengthened; for when she mentions whom she is seeking, her love is kindled all the more ardently.

Jesus says to her: Mary. Jesus is not recognized when he calls her "woman"; so he calls her by name, as though he were saying: Recognize me as I recognize you; for I do not know you as I know others; I know you as yourself. And so Mary, once addressed by name, recognizes who is speaking. She immediately calls him *rabboni,* that is to say, *teacher,* because the one whom she sought outwardly was the one who inwardly taught her to keep on searching.

All my hope lies in your great mercy

Augustine: *Confessions*

WHERE did I find you, that I came to know you? You were not within my memory before I learned of you. Where, then, did I find you before I came to know you, if not within yourself, far above me? We come to you and go from you, but no place is involved in this process. In every place, O Truth, you are present to those who seek your help, and at once and the same time you answer all, though they seek your counsel on different matters.

You respond clearly, but not everyone hears clearly. All ask what they wish, but do not always hear the answer they wish. Your best servant is he who is intent not so much on hearing his petition answered, as rather on willing whatever he hears from you.

Late have I loved you, O Beauty ever ancient, ever new, late have I loved you! You were within me, but I was outside, and it was there that I searched for you. In my unloveliness I plunged into the lovely things which you created. You were with me, but I was not with you. Created things kept me from you; yet if they had not been in you they would not have been at all. You called, you shouted, and you broke through my deafness. You flashed your fragrance on me; I drew in breath and now I pant for you. I have tasted you; now I hunger and thirst for more. You touched me, and I burned for your peace.

When once I shall be united to you with my whole being, I shall at last be free of sorrow and toil. Then my life will be alive, filled entirely with you. When you fill someone, you relieve him of his burden, but because I am not yet filled with you, I am a burden to myself. My joy when I should be weeping struggles with my sorrows when I should be rejoicing. I know not where victory lies. Woe is me! Lord, have mercy on me! My evil sorrows and good joys are at war with one another. I know not where victory lies. Woe is me! Lord, have mercy! Woe is me! I make no effort to conceal my wounds. You are my physician, I am your patient. You are merciful; I stand in need of mercy.

God's temple is holy; you are his temple

Ambrose: *Exposition of Psalm 118*

MY FATHER and I will come and make our home with him: Let your door stand open to receive him, unlock your soul to him, offer him a welcome in your mind, and then you will see the riches of simplicity, the treasures of peace, the joy of grace. Throw wide the gate of your heart, stand before the sun of the everlasting light *that shines on every man.* This true light shines on all, but if anyone closes his window he will deprive himself of eternal light. If you shut the door of your mind, you shut out Christ. Though he can enter, he does not want to force his way in rudely, or compel us to admit him against our will.

Born of a virgin, he came forth from the womb as the light of the whole world in order to shine on all men. His light is received by those who long for the splendor of perpetual light that night can never destroy. The sun of our daily experience is succeeded by the darkness of night, but the sun of holiness never sets, because wisdom cannot give place to evil.

Blessed then is the man at whose door Christ stands and knocks. Our door is faith; if it is strong enough, the whole house is safe. This is the door by which Christ enters. So the Church says in the Song of Songs: *The voice of my brother is at the door.* Hear his knock, listen to him asking to enter: *Open to me, my sister, my betrothed, my dove, my perfect one, for my head is covered with dew, and my hair with the moisture of the night.*

When does God the Word most often knock at your door?—When his head is covered with the dew of night. He visits in love those in trouble and temptation to save them from being overwhelmed by their trials. His head is covered with dew or moisture when those who are his body are in distress. That is the time when you must keep watch so that when the bridegroom comes he may not find himself shut out, and take his departure. If you were to sleep, if your heart were not wide awake, he would not knock but go away; but if your heart is watchful, he knocks and asks you to open the door to him.

Our soul has a door; it has gates. *Lift up your heads, O gates, and be lifted up, eternal gates, and the King of glory will enter.* If you open the gates of your faith, the King of glory will enter your house in the triumphal procession in honor of his passion. Holiness too has its gates. We read in Scripture what the Lord Jesus said through his prophet: *Open for me the gates of holiness.*

It is the soul that has its door, its gates. Christ comes to this door and knocks; he knocks at these gates. Open to him; he wants to enter, to find his bride waiting and watching.

The living water of the Holy Spirit

Cyril of Jerusalem: *Catechetical Instruction*

THE water that I shall give him will become in him a fountain of living water, welling up into eternal life. This is a new kind of water, a living, leaping water, welling up for those who are worthy. But why did Christ call the grace of the Spirit water? Because all things are dependent on water; plants and animals have their origin in water. Water comes down from heaven as rain, and although it is always the same in itself, it produces many different effects, one in the palm tree, another in the vine, and so on throughout the whole of creation. It does not come down, now as one thing, now as another, but while remaining essentially the same, it adapts itself to the needs of every creature that receives it.

In the same way the Holy Spirit, whose nature is always the same, simple and indivisible, apportions grace to each man as he wills. Like a dry tree which puts forth shoots when watered, the soul bears the fruit of holiness when repentance has made it worthy of receiving the Holy Spirit. Although the Spirit never changes, the effects of his action, by the will of God and in the name of Christ, are both many and marvelous.

The Spirit makes one man a teacher of divine truth, inspires another to prophesy, gives another the power of casting out devils, enables another to interpret holy Scripture. The Spirit strengthens one man's self-control, shows another how to help the poor, teaches another to fast and lead a life of asceticism, makes another oblivious to the needs of the body, trains another for martyrdom. His action is different in different people, but the Spirit himself is always the same. *In each person,* Scripture says, *the Spirit reveals his presence in a particular way for the common good.*

The Spirit comes gently and makes himself known by his fragrance. He is not felt as a burden, for he is light, very light. Rays of light and knowledge stream before him as he approaches. The Spirit comes with the tenderness of a true friend and protector to save, to heal, to teach, to counsel, to strengthen, to console. The Spirit comes to enlighten the mind first of the one who receives him, and then, through him, the minds of others as well.

As light strikes the eyes of a man who comes out of darkness into the sunshine and enables him to see clearly things he could not discern before, so light floods the soul of the man counted worthy of receiving the Holy Spirit and enables him to see things beyond the range of human vision, things hitherto undreamed of.

Devotion must be practiced in different ways

Francis de Sales: *Introduction to the Devout Life*

WHEN God the Creator made all things, he commanded the plants to bring forth fruit each according to its own kind; he has likewise commanded Christians, who are the living plants of his Church, to bring forth the fruits of devotion, each one in accord with his character, his station and his calling.

I say that devotion must be practiced in different ways by the nobleman and by the working man, by the servant and by the prince, by the widow, by the unmarried girl and by the married woman. But even this distinction is not sufficient; for the practice of devotion must be adapted to the strength, to the occupation and to the duties of each one in particular.

Tell me, please, my Philothea, whether it is proper for a bishop to want to lead a solitary life like a Carthusian; or for married people to be no more concerned than a Capuchin about increasing their income; or for a working man to spend his whole day in church like a religious; or on the other hand for a religious to be constantly exposed like a bishop to all the events and circumstances that bear on the needs of our neighbor. Is not this sort of devotion ridiculous, unorganized and intolerable? Yet this absurd error occurs very frequently, but in no way does true devotion, my Philothea, destroy anything at all. On the contrary, it perfects and fulfills all things. In fact if it ever works against, or is inimical to, anyone's legitimate station and calling, then it is very definitely false devotion.

The bee collects honey from flowers in such a way as to do the least damage or destruction to them, and he leaves them whole, undamaged and fresh, just as he found them. True devotion does still better. Not only does it not injure any sort of calling or occupation, it even embellishes and enhances it.

Moreover, just as every sort of gem, cast in honey, becomes brighter and more sparkling, each according to its color, so each person becomes more acceptable and fitting in his own vocation when he sets his vocation in the context of devotion. Through devotion your family cares become more peaceful, mutual love between husband and wife becomes more sincere, the service we owe to the prince becomes more faithful, and our work, no matter what it is, becomes more pleasant and agreeable.

In the heart of the Church I will be love

Theresa of the Child Jesus: *Autobiography*

SINCE my longing for martyrdom was powerful and unsettling, I turned to the epistles of Saint Paul in the hope of finally finding an answer. By chance the twelfth and thirteenth chapters of the first epistle to the Corinthians caught my attention, and in the first section I read that not everyone can be an apostle, prophet or teacher, that the Church is composed of a variety of members, and that the eye cannot be the hand. Even with such an answer revealed before me, I was not satisfied and did not find peace.

I persevered in the reading and did let not my mind wander until I found this encouraging theme: *Set your desires on the greater gifts. And I will now show you the way which surpasses all others.* For the Apostle insists that the greater gifts are nothing at all without love and that this same love is surely the best path leading directly to God. At length I had found peace of mind.

When I had looked upon the mystical body of the Church, I recognized myself in none of the members which Saint Paul described, and what is more, I desired to distinguish myself more favorably within the whole body. Love appeared to me to be the hinge for my vocation. Indeed I knew that the Church had a body composed of various members, but in this body the necessary and more noble member was not lacking; I knew that the Church had a heart and that such a heart appeared to be aflame with love. I knew that one love drove the members of the Church to action, that if this love were extinguished, the apostles would have proclaimed the Gospel no longer, the martyrs would have shed their blood no more. I saw and realized that love sets off the bounds of all vocations, that love is everything, that this same love embraces every time and every place. In one word, that love is everlasting.

Then, nearly ecstatic with the supreme joy in my soul, I proclaimed: O Jesus, my love, at last I have found my calling: my call is love. Certainly I have found my proper place in the Church, and you gave me that very place, my God. In the heart of the Church, my mother, I will be love, and thus I will be all things, as my desire finds its direction.

PRAYERS

Prayer to Jesus Crucified

LORD Jesus Christ,
I thank you, who laid down your life for me so meekly.
You bore the nails so patiently,
you were raised upon the cross so mercifully,
you hung there so painfully,
you wept so bitterly,
you cried aloud piercingly,
you shed your blood plentifully,
and for me, a sinner, you suffered death unquestionably.

Now, Lord Jesus Christ,
I commend myself to your love,
to the power of your passion,
to the depths of your endless mercy.

Jesus Christ,
in your immeasurable pity,
keep alive within me the memory
of your bitter death,
of your holy wounds,
so that in sickness and in health,
I may remember your mercy.

Gentle Jesus,
defend me from all danger,
and keep me so that I may stand before you in joy.
Defend my soul, Lord Jesus Christ,
which you have bought with your precious blood. Amen.

Prayer of St. Patrick

CHRIST be with me, Christ before me, Christ behind me, Christ in me, Christ beneath me, Christ above me, Christ on my right, Christ on my left, Christ where I lie, Christ where I arise, Christ in the heart of everyone who thinks of me, Christ in the mouth of everyone who speaks of me, Christ in every eye that sees me, Christ in every ear that hears me. In the Name of the Father and of the Son and of the Holy Spirit. Amen.

Prayer of St. Francis of Assisi

LORD, make me an instrument of thy peace.
Where there is hatred, let me sow love.
Where there is injury, pardon.
Where there is doubt, faith.
Where there is despair, hope.
Where there is darkness, light.
Where there is sadness, joy.

O Divine Master, grant that I may not
so much seek to be consoled as to console
to be understood as to understand
to be loved as to love.
For it is in giving that we receive;
it is in pardoning that we are pardoned;
it is in dying that we are born to eternal life.

The Canticle of Brother Sun

Leader: Antiphon: Let all there is give you thanks and praise.

1. Most high, all-powerful, all-good, Lord! All praise is yours, all glory, all honor and all blessing.

2. To you, alone, Most High, do they belong. No mortal lips are worthy to pronounce your name.

1. All praise be yours, my Lord, through all that you have made, and first my lord Brother Sun, who brings the day; and light you give to us through him.

2. How beautiful is he, how radiant in all his splendor! Of you, Most High, he bears the likeness.

1. All praise be yours, my Lord, through Sister Moon and the Stars; in the heavens you have made them bright and precious and fair.

2. All praise be yours, my Lord, through Brothers Wind and Air, and fair and stormy, all the weather's moods, by which you cherish all that you have made.

1. All praise be yours, my Lord, through Sister Water, so useful, lowly, precious and pure.

2. All praise be yours, my Lord, through Brother Fire, through whom you brighten up the night. How beautiful is he, how gay! Full of power and strength.

1. All praise be yours, my Lord, through Sister Earth, our mother, who feeds us in her sovereignty and produces various fruits with colored flowers and herbs.

2. All praise be yours, my Lord, through those who grant pardon for love of you; through those who endure sickness and trial.

1. Happy those who endure in peace, by you, Most High, they will be crowned.

2. All praise be yours, my Lord, through Sister Death, from whose embrace no mortal can escape.

1. Woe to those who die in mortal sin! Happy those she finds doing your will! The second death can do no harm to them.

2. Praise and bless my Lord, and give him thanks, and serve him with great humility.

Prayer of St. Thomas Aquinas

I THANK you, O holy Lord, almighty Father, eternal God, who have deigned, not through any merit of mine, but out of the condescension of your goodness, to nourish me a sinner, your unworthy servant, with the Precious Body and Blood of your Son, our Lord Jesus Christ.

I pray that this Holy Communion be not a condemnation to punishment for me, but a saving plea unto forgiveness.

May it be unto me the armor of faith and the shield of a good will. May it be the emptying out of my vices and the extinction of all lustful desires; an increase of charity and patience, of humility and obedience; and of all virtues; a strong defense against the snares of all my enemies, visible and invisible; the perfect quieting of all my evil impulses of flesh and spirit, binding me firmly to you, the one true God; and a happy ending of my life.

I pray too that you will deign to bring me a sinner to that ineffable banquet, where you with your Son and the Holy Spirit, are to your saints true light, fulfillment of desires, eternal joy, gladness without end, and perfect bliss. Through Christ our Lord.

Anima Christi

SOUL of Christ, sanctify me,
Body of Christ, save me,
Blood of Christ, fill me,
Water from the side of Christ, wash me.
Passion of Christ, strengthen me,
O good Jesus, hear me.
Within your wounds hide me,
Permit me not to be separated from you.
From the wicked foe defend me,
At the hour of my death call me
And bid me come to you,
That with your saints I may praise you,
Forever and ever. Amen.

Take and Receive

St. Ignatius

TAKE, Lord, and receive all my liberty,
my memory, my understanding and my entire will,
all I have and call my own.
You have given all to me.
To you, Lord, I return it.
Everything is yours; do with it what you will.
Give me only your love and your grace,
that is enough for me.

Prayer for Generosity

St. Ignatius

LORD, teach me to be generous.
Teach me to serve you as you deserve.
To give and not to count the cost.
To fight and not to heed the wounds.
To toil and not to seek for rest.
To labor and not ask for reward,
Save that of knowing I am doing your will.

Prayer to Jesus Crucified

St. Francis Xavier

O GOD, thou art the object of my love, not for the hope of endless joys above, nor for the fear of endless pain below which those who love thee not must undergo.

For me and such as me, thou once didst bear the shameful cross, the nails, the spear. A thorny crown transpierced thy sacred brow. What bloody sweat from every member flowed. Such then was—and is—thy love for me. Such is—and shall be still—my love for thee.

Prayer of Cardinal Newman

LORD Jesus, help me to spread your fragrance everywhere I go. Flood my soul with your spirit and life. Penetrate and possess my whole being so utterly that my life may only be a radiance of you. Shine through me and be so in me that every soul I come in contact with may feel your presence and your spirit.

Let them look up and see only Jesus. Stay with me and I shall shine as you shine, so as to be a light to others. Lord Jesus, let me praise you in the way you love best: by radiating you to those around me. Let me preach the Gospel with my whole life: the overflow of the love my heart bears to you. Amen.

I Have a Mission

Blessed Cardinal Newman

O MY God, you have created me to do some definite service. You have committed some work to me which you have not committed to another. I have my mission, I am a link in a chain, a bond of connection between persons. You have not created me for nothing. Therefore I will trust you, whatever, wherever I am. If I am in sickness, my sickness may serve you. If I am in perplexity, my perplexity may serve you.

If I am in sorrow, my sorrow may serve you. You do nothing in vain. You know what you are about. Though friends be taken away, though I feel desolate, though my spirits sink, though my future is hidden from me, yet will I trust you for you know what you are about. I ask not so much to see as to be used: through Christ our Lord. Amen.

Prayer of Abandonment

Charles de Foucauld

FATHER, I abandon myself into your hands; do with me whatever you will. Whatever you may do, I thank you. I am ready for all, I accept all. Let only your will be done in me, and in all your creatures. I wish no more than this, O Lord. Into your hands I commend my spirit; I offer it to you with all the love of my heart, for I do love you, Lord, and so need to give myself, to surrender myself into your hands, without reserve and with boundless confidence, for you are my Father.

Litany to St. Alphonsus

ST. ALPHONSUS, hospital minister to the incurably ill who learned compassion in service to others, pray for us!

For with the Lord is kindness, and with him is plenteous redemption.

St. Alphonsus, who spread God's tender love through street preaching and through creation of an association of evening chapels, pray for us!

For with the Lord is kindness, and with him is plenteous redemption.

St. Alphonsus, spiritual director who gently encouraged sinners to repent and pray and who deeply challenged good people to become saints, pray for us!

For with the Lord is kindness, and with him is plenteous redemption.

St. Alphonsus, man of letters whose pamphlets and books reveal in simple language the good news of God's redeeming love, pray for us!

For with the Lord is kindness, and with him is plenteous redemption.

St. Alphonsus, mystic who found God to be father, mother, sister, brother, lover and dearest friend, pray for us!

For with the Lord is kindness, and with him is plenteous redemption.

St. Alphonsus, founder of Redemptorist missionaries whose spirit lives in generations of Redemptorists, Redemptoristines and Immaculate Heart of Mary Congregations, pray for us!

For with the Lord is kindness, and with him is plenteous redemption.

St. Alphonsus, friend of the poor who shared all you had while living in need yourself, pray for us!

For with the Lord is kindness, and with him is plenteous redemption.

St. Alphonsus, superior general who served your brothers on good days and bad, pray for us!

For with the Lord is kindness, and with him is plenteous redemption.

St. Alphonsus, canonized saint, Doctor of prayer, patron of moralists and confessors, artist, musician, poet, nobleman and lawyer, filled with the Spirit of God in spite of human weaknesses, pray for us!

For with the Lord is kindness, and with him is plenteous redemption.

St. Alphonsus, Doctor of the Church who teaches us how to pray, to serve, to forgive and to love, pray for us!

For with the Lord is kindness, and with him is plenteous redemption.

The Te Deum

YOU are God: we praise you;
You are the Lord: we acclaim you;
You are the eternal Father:
All creation worships you.

To you all angels, all the powers of heaven,
Cherubim and Seraphim, sing in endless praise:
  Holy, holy, holy, Lord, God of power and might,
  heaven and earth are full of your glory.

The glorious company of apostles praise you.
The noble fellowship of prophets praise you.
The white-robed army of martyrs praise you.

Throughout the world the holy Church acclaims you:
  Father, of majesty unbounded,
  your true and only Son, worthy of all worship,
  and the Holy Spirit, advocate and guide.

You, Christ, are the king of glory,
the eternal Son of the Father.

When you became man to set us free
you did not spurn the Virgin's womb.

You overcame the sting of death,
and opened the kingdom of heaven to all believers.

You are seated at God's right hand in glory.
We believe that you will come, and be our judge.

Come then, Lord, and help your people,
bought with the price of your own blood,
and bring us with your saints
to glory everlasting.

PENITENTIAL SERVICES

1

(Extracted from the Rite of Penance)

TEXTS FOR THE PENITENT

The penitent should prepare for the celebration of the sacrament by prayer, reading of Scripture, and silent reflection. The penitent should think over and should regret all sins since the last celebration of the sacrament.

Reception of the Penitent

The penitent enters the confessional or other place set aside for the celebration of the sacrament of penance. After the welcoming of the priest, the penitent makes the sign of the cross, saying:

In the name of the Father, and of the Son, and of the Holy Spirit. Amen.

The penitent is invited to have trust in God and replies:

Amen.

Reading of the Word of God

The penitent then listens to a text of Scripture which tells about God's mercy and calls man to conversion.

Confession of Sins and Acceptance of Satisfaction

The penitent tells the priest when he or she last celebrated the sacrament, and then confesses his or her sins, asking appropriate questions if necessary. The penitent then listens to any advice the priest may give and accepts the satisfaction (or "penance") from the priest.

Prayer of the Penitent and Absolution

Prayer

Before the absolution is given, the penitent expresses sorrow for sins in these or similar words:

My God,
I am sorry for my sins with all my heart.
In choosing to do wrong
and failing to do good,
I have sinned against you
whom I should love above all things.
I firmly intend, with your help,
to do penance,
to sin no more,
and to avoid whatever leads me to sin.
Our Savior Jesus Christ
suffered and died for us.
In his name, my God, have mercy.

OR

Remember that your compassion, O LORD,
  and your love are from of old.
In your kindness remember me,
  because of your goodness, O LORD.

OR

Thoroughly wash me from my guilt
  and of my sin cleanse me.
For I acknowledge my offense,
  and my sin is before me always.

OR

Father, I have sinned [. . .] against you.
I no longer deserve to be called your son.
Be merciful to me a sinner.

OR

Father of mercy,
like the prodigal son

I return to you and say:
"I have sinned against you
and am no longer worthy to be called your son."
Christ Jesus, Savior of the world,
I pray with the repentant thief
to whom you promised Paradise:
"Lord, remember me in your kingdom."
Holy Spirit, fountain of love,
I call on you with trust:
"Purify my heart,
and help me to walk as a child of light."

OR

Lord Jesus,
you opened the eyes of the blind,
healed the sick,
forgave the sinful woman,
and after Peter's denial confirmed him in your love.
Listen to my prayer:
forgive all my sins,
renew your love in my heart,
help me to live in perfect unity with my fellow Christians
that I may proclaim your saving power to all the world.

OR

Lord Jesus,
you chose to be called the friend of sinners.
By your saving death and resurrection
free me from my sins.
May your peace take root in my heart
and bring forth a harvest
of love, holiness, and truth.

OR

Lord Jesus Christ,
you are the Lamb of God;
you take away the sins of the world.
Through the grace of the Holy Spirit
restore me to friendship with your Father,
cleanse me from every stain of sin
in the blood you shed for me,
and raise me to new life
for the glory of your name.

OR

Lord God,
in your goodness have mercy on me:
do not look on my sins,
but take away all my guilt.
Create in me a clean heart
and renew within me an upright spirit.

OR

Lord Jesus, Son of God,
have mercy on me, a sinner.

Absolution

If the penitent is not kneeling, he or she bows his or her head. The priest extends his hands (or at least extends his right hand} and says:

God, the Father of mercies,
through the death and resurrection of his Son
has reconciled the world to himself
and sent the Holy Spirit among us
for the forgiveness of sins;
through the ministry of the Church
may God give you pardon and peace,

and I absolve you from your sins
in the name of the Father, and of the Son, ✠
and of the Holy Spirit.

The penitent answers:

Amen.

Proclamation of Praise of God and Dismissal

Penitent and priest give praise to God.

Priest: Give thanks to the Lord, for he is good.
Penitent: His mercy endures for ever.

Then the penitent is dismissed by the priest.

Priest: The Lord has freed you from your sins. Go in peace.

2

CALL TO PRAYER:

Leader: This is a day of true repentance, a time to return to God with all our hearts.

ALL: We return to God in true repentance for all those things which we have done that we should not have done and for those things we have left undone which we should have done.

Leader: We seek God's forgiveness.

ALL: We affirm that God is gracious and merciful, slow to anger and abounding in steadfast love.

INSTRUCTION

PRESIDER'S PRAYER:

Loving God, you know our weakness and the extent of our failure to love you and one another.

You see the sincerity of our efforts as well. Look upon us who have been offended and lift up our hearts. Look upon us who have given offense and help us heal the hurt we have caused. As we willingly, with your help, forgive one another, we ask you to forgive us and fill us with your healing power and grace. Amen.

SCRIPTURE READING:

REFLECTIVE SILENCE

LITANY OF REPENTANCE: (Please kneel)

ALL: Loving God, you are just and compassionate; be with us today. We look to the future, to the days ahead of us, and yet we know we have need already of forgiveness and healing.

RIGHT: We ask forgiveness of you, our God, and the forgiveness of those gathered here, for becoming impatient when we were too busy, too distracted, too much in a hurry.

LEFT: We ask forgiveness for being too quick to speak or act, for not taking time to think or pray.

RIGHT: We ask forgiveness for falling into the same mistakes again and again, which cause hurt to others and to ourselves.

LEFT: We ask forgiveness for taking too much time, for wasting time before we act, for being concerned about appearances and approval, for not trusting in your own absolute love for us.

RIGHT: We ask forgiveness for the smallness of mind in our thoughts, for a narrowness of heart in our actions. Help us to accept others who think and act differently from us.

LEFT: We ask forgiveness for letting fatigue discourage us, for becoming cynical about the worth of our own efforts and the power of your grace, for minimizing the urgency of the Gospel.

SCRIPTURE READING:

RESPONSE: (All stand for Sprinkling Rite)

Concluding Prayer

LOVING God, your Son Jesus brings forgiveness to our broken world through his death on the cross. Through Jesus, you plead for our wholehearted return to you. Open our ears to your call. Help us to see our need for reconciliation and peace within ourselves, with one another, and with our world. Rend our hearts with the power of your Word as we take the first step in turning to you for forgiveness.

Individual Reception of the Sacrament of Reconciliation

From *More Than Words* by Janet Schaffran and Pat Kozak

3

OPENING SONG:
OPENING PRAYER:

Leader: Merciful God, our shelter and our refuge. We come before you today to reflect on our common sinfulness and to ask your pardon and peace for all the wrongs we have committed. We ask you to be merciful and trust that you will lead us on the proper path that we should follow in being your disciples. We trust in your mercy this day, in Jesus' name.

ALL: Amen.

READING AND EXAMINATION OF CONSCIENCE: (based on Matt. 5: 1-12)

Leader: Having placed ourselves before God let us now listen to his word.

Seeing the crowds, he went up the hill. There he sat down and was joined by his disciples. Then he began to speak. This is what he taught them: How happy are the poor in spirit: theirs is the kingdom of heaven. Happy the gentle: they shall have the earth for their heritage. Happy those who mourn: they shall be comforted. Happy those who hunger and thirst for what is right: they shall be satisfied. Happy the merciful: they shall have mercy shown them. Happy the pure in heart: they shall see God. Happy the peacemakers: they shall be called sons of God. Happy those who are persecuted in the cause of right: theirs is the kingdom of heaven. Happy are you when people abuse you and persecute you and speak all kinds of calumny against you on my account. Rejoice and be glad, for your reward will be great in heaven: this is how they persecuted the prophets before you.

(Pause for Silent Reflection)

Leader: Let us now use the eight beatitudes that Jesus said describe his followers in order to examine our conscience, and ask for forgiveness.

Blessed are you, God our Creator, for giving your kingdom to the poor in spirit:

ALL: Forgive us for the times / we have forgotten that you are our creator / and have tried to pretend we are like you / and can do everything ourselves / and not depend on you.

SUNG RESPONSE: (As above.)

Leader: Blessed are you, O God for giving the earth as an inheritance to the humble:

ALL: Forgive us for our arrogance and self-centeredness / in selfishly going after the things of this earth / while hurting others to get what we want / and to have our own way.

SUNG RESPONSE: (As above.)

Leader: Blessed are you, Father, for comforting those who mourn:

ALL: Forgive us for the times we have failed to comfort others / who have come to us in need / pardon us for failing to extend our love to the less fortunate.

SUNG RESPONSE: (As above.)

Leader: Blessed are you, O Lord, for satisfying those who hunger and thirst for justice:

ALL: Forgive us for our lack of honesty / for taking what was not ours / and for forgetting the basic rights of all. / Pardon us for always wanting more and more / while others lack the basics. / Pardon us for wasting our precious resources.

SUNG RESPONSE: (As above.)

Leader: Forgive us for the times we have failed to forgive others. / Pardon us for passing judgment on others / and for the enjoyment we took in criticizing others.

SUNG RESPONSE: (As above.)

Leader: Blessed are you, O Lord, for revealing yourself to the pure of heart:

ALL: Forgive us for the times we have made war in our hearts. / Pardon us for brooding over hurts and grievances. / Forgive us for self-pity and needless anxiety.

SUNG RESPONSE: (As above.)

Leader: Blessed are you, O Lord, for giving the kingdom of heaven to those who are persecuted in the cause of right:

ALL: Forgive us for fleeing the suffering / that is necessary when loving others. / Pardon us for persecuting in our hearts and actions / those who are different than ourselves. / Forgive us for not living out your commandments / for fear of being persecuted as Jesus was.

SUNG RESPONSE: (As above.)

Leader: In these many ways we have become dead in sin, but the Lord always brings us back to life with His Son, Jesus, who has taught us how to pray as God's children; so we say:

ALL: Our Father . . .

Leader: Let us now offer each other a sign of Christ's peace. (All exchange a sign of peace.)

Individual confessions are now available. Music will be played in the chapel area for prayer and penance. We will not reassemble so that all may have private time for prayer and reflection.

DATES OF RETREATS

DATES OF RETREATS

ISBN 978-1-953152-56-5
90000
9 781953 152565